Contents

Good Dogs
Doing Good

Lives Transformed by Man's Best Friend

Edited by

Richard Day Gore and Juliann Garey

LaChancepublishing

LACHANCE PUBLISHING • NEW YORK

12577617

Copyright © 2010 by LaChance Publishing LLC

ISBN 978-1-934184-09-7

Victor Starsia
Publisher

Richard Day Gore
Senior Editor

Juliann Garey
Associate Editor

Library of Congress Control Number: 2009931880

Publisher: LaChance Publishing LLC
               120 Bond Street
               Brooklyn, NY 11217
               www.lachancepublishing.com

Distributor: Independent Publishers Group
               814 North Franklin Street
               Chicago, IL 60610
               www.ipgbook.com

This book is available at special discounts for bulk purchases for sales promotions or premiums. Special editions, including personalized covers, excerpts of existing books, and corporate imprints, can be created in large quantities for special needs. For more information, write to LaChance Publishing, 120 Bond Street, New York, NY 11217 or email info@lachancepublishing.com.

Introduction

"Good dog!"

Who knows who first shouted this phrase, or when, or where, or in what language.

The story of dogs is, in some ways, the story of humankind. Dogs have been the intimate companions to humans for thousands of years. While it is likely that the bond between man and dog had practical origins (hunting, herding and protection) it is easy to imagine that even the most primitive man and woman enjoyed the simpler pleasures of this most loyal—and in some respects most human-seeming—of animals. No one knows who first recognized the friendly meaning of a wagging tail, or when the first stick was thrown, brought back, and thrown again. But the intimacy shared between man and dog seems to be integral to both: man and dog have been making each other smile since time immemorial.

Whether for companionship or survival, the company of dogs has been vital to the well being of countless individuals, families, tribes and cultures throughout history. Some anthropologists believe that sled dogs made it possible for ancient settlers to cross the Bering Strait. The ancient Romans believed that, as helpless infants, the founders of Rome, Romulus and Remus, were protected and fed by a wild wolf. Egyptian tombs feature magnificent depictions of the hallowed stature of dogs in that culture. Hunters, prospectors and settlers used their dogs for warmth and protection against the elements (the origin of the expression "three-dog night"). It's no surprise then, that through the millennia people have honored the humble dog as hero, friend, family member, companion.

Just as in the past, dogs in today's world continue to make themselves valuable to us in ways far beyond making us smile and laugh. For decades, dogs have been trained to lead the blind and to assist the deaf. More recently, therapy dogs have helped lead many individuals into more rewarding lives, whether by providing non-judgmental companionship to children with developmental difficulties or by giving solace to the ill and housebound.

The movies have always been full of dogs that swim the raging river to rescue the child, or dash into the burning house to save the family. But it is no less heroic for a dog to inspire a gravely ill child to see beyond his difficulties and begin healing. Or to help a young woman banish her anger and depression at her inability to bear a child. Or to show a teacher how to reach and save the most unreachable, troubled student. The stars of *Good Dogs Doing Good* are just as remarkable and heroic as the sled dogs that helped ancient man find new worlds, or the death-defying canines of the movies. They personify the qualities of loyalty, patience, determination, humor, nobility and industry that have been the building blocks of our relationship with canines since the dawn of time. Perhaps that is what draws man to dogs so strongly and poignantly: they embody the best traits we wish to see in ourselves. This inspiring collection of true stories, written by people from all walks of life and from around the world, pays moving homage to dogs that have, in their own ways, given hope to those with none, helped teach valuable lessons both large and small about the human condition, and allowed others to gain new perspectives on their own lives and the lives of others. They amply demonstrate how the humble dog continues to earn his nickname, "man's best friend."

Richard Day Gore

Teacher's Pet

M. Molly Backes

Zeke was a bad dog. The first time I saw him, he was streaking across a campus quad, ears flying in the wind, leash dragging behind him, while his owner chased after him on a bike, screaming his name. "Zeke! ZEKE! Bad dog!"

Zeke lived across the street from my family's home during my last year of college, and I watched him, surreptitiously, from my porch. Sometimes I stopped on my way home to pet him. My dog had died the year before and my mom had gotten herself a new dog, but the dog your family gets when you are twenty-one and in school is not the same as the one they get when you are ten and lonely and in need of a best friend. I patted Zeke on the head, gingerly, because his dull brown fur was sticky and dusted with dandruff. He had amber eyes and a stump for a tail and an extreme arthritic limp that didn't prevent him from running away every chance he got. It became routine: Zeke ran away and his owner chased him on his bike, screaming and cursing. "Bad, bad dog!"

Sometimes I saw the man go after Zeke with a stick, yelling and hitting him. Once I tried to talk to the man about it, asking if it was really necessary to hit the dog. "Oh yes," he said. "He is a very bad dog. How else will he learn?" Politeness and fear trapped me in silence, and I shrugged unhappily. "In this country, you treat your dogs better than people," he said. "In my country, dogs are for working."

Zeke

I told myself it was a cultural difference and not my place to interfere. Still, I flinched whenever I saw the man hitting Zeke. Even if he was a bad dog.

Eventually I graduated, moved across town, and began student teaching in a seventh grade classroom. The ten-year difference in age between my students and me felt like nothing. Trent Kidder sat in the last row of my last class of the day, and he was a problem from the first.

"Oh, Trent Kidder," the other teachers said knowingly. "He's a bad kid."

The other teachers told me I needed to be harsh with Trent, show him who was boss. They told me never to smile. They told me to send him to the principal right off the bat, to establish my dominance. I followed their advice, but Trent just got worse and worse. After school every day I went back to campus where I attended methods classes and wrote research papers and thought about how to tone Trent down and spice up my lessons so the rest of my students would care about class.

One Thursday afternoon in early September, my old neighbor showed up at my door with Zeke. It was an emergency, he said. He had to go out of town for the weekend and there wasn't anyone else. Could I please take the dog, just until Sunday night?

"I'm sorry," I said. I couldn't do it; my landlord had a very strict policy against dogs.

"Please," the man said. "You're the only one."

I looked down. Zeke was wearing an ill-fitting red harness that cut under his legs and across his neck. He looked uncomfortable. "Oh, all right. Just until Sunday."

When he was gone, I looked at Zeke. "I guess you're stuck with me, buddy." Zeke wagged his stump.

In my family, we'd always left the dog food out all day, and the dogs would eat when they were hungry. I put out a bowl of food for Zeke and he gobbled it as if he didn't know when he'd see his next meal. Taken aback, I filled his bowl again, and he immediately finished it. "Hey," I said. "I'll feed you every day. I promise." I washed him and brushed him but my family was not impressed. "What a dirty old dog," they said. "He's so old! He probably won't live through the weekend."

"He's not dirty," I insisted.

On Sunday, I waited for Zeke's owner. I read a book, and Zeke slept at my feet. The minutes ticked by. I read another book. The man didn't come. Finally at ten o'clock he called me and said he wasn't going to make it. He was in Atlanta. "What am I supposed to do?" I demanded. "I can't keep him!" The man begged me. Just one week. Please. Next

Sunday. He promised. What could I do? I said fine and hung up. Zeke wagged his stump and went back to sleep.

I spent the week sneaking around, trying to keep him hidden. I left him in the basement during the day and took him to campus with me when I could, letting him curl up at my feet in the curriculum library after everyone else had gone home for the night. He panicked when I left, and broke out of every kind of barrier I could make. When I was home, he stayed close to me, winding himself between my legs as I walked through the house and sneaking under the covers at night, like he thought I would leave if he let me out of his sight.

> "Zeke ran away and his owner chased him on his bike, screaming and cursing. 'Bad, bad dog!'"

His owner called again Sunday night. From New York this time. No, he couldn't come get him. Maybe next week.

I took Zeke to the vet and got him glucosamine, and he stopped limping. I brushed him every day and fed him eggs to make his coat soft and shiny brown. I talked to the people who knew his owner, followed a trail through his past to learn as much as I could about him. In the last year, the man had already left Zeke with three other families.

The next week, he didn't come back, and he didn't call.

My mother the social worker said Zeke reminded her of the foster children she'd worked with over the years. She put him in her car to take him on a play date and said he looked like a foster kid, resigned to the fact that she would leave him again, that no one wanted to be his forever family.

After six weeks, we got an envelope in the mail with Zeke's medical records and a note from one of Zeke's previous foster homes. The note said, *Congratulations on your new dog!* "I thought you were dog-sitting him," my mother said. I looked down at Zeke, who stood leaning against my legs. He wagged his stump at me. "I guess not."

A few weeks after that, a friend of mine yelled at him as a joke. "Bad dog!" he yelled, and Zeke cowered in fear, whimpering. I nearly kicked my friend out of the house. "Don't you ever yell at my dog again." I knelt down and wrapped my arms around him, shushing him. "You're safe," I told him. "You'll always be safe with me. I promise you."

I fed him every day and though he always ate with relish, he lost that haunted look that said he didn't know when he'd get his next meal. Our family vet helped perfect his glucosamine dosage until his limp disappeared altogether. I walked him every day and let him sleep next to me with his head on the pillow at night.

Zeke became a very good dog.

Little kids could hit him on the head and he'd just stand there, smiling his doggy smile and wagging his stump. I took him to visit my elderly relatives and saw decades drop from their faces as they stroked his soft ears. He was my co-pilot, my hiking buddy, my muse, my partner in crime, my entertainment when I was bored, my relief after a long day at school. My best friend.

Trent, on the other hand, got worse and worse. He interrupted my class at every opportunity, and started to rally the other kids to his cause, until I worried about mutiny. One day I watched him running around the field at lunch, and thought of the first time I saw Zeke—of his unfettered glee as he flew across the quad. The advice of the other teachers suddenly reminded me of what the man had told me about Zeke: "How else will he learn?" I thought about the light that came into Zeke's eyes, slowly, after months of care and love. Hitting him with a stick made him bad. Treating him with gentle care made him good.

So I forgot the advice of the veteran teachers and followed a hunch instead. Rather than showing Trent who was boss by punishing him, I waited until a day when he was less obnoxious than usual and pounced.

"You did such a great job today!" I told him. "You're a leader in the class, and the other kids look up to you."

I saw a tiny light appear in Trent's eyes. "Really?"

"Absolutely," I said, and smiled at him. By the end of the semester, Trent was a model student—but only in my class. The other teachers still complained about him and asked me what my secret was.

"I just told him he was a good person, and he blossomed." Maybe that's all any of us needs, really: someone to pat us on the back and tell us we're doing a good job.

Nine months after he left, the man reappeared and tried to reclaim Zeke, acting as if that was the plan all along. Though I'm the least confrontational person in the world, I stood my ground, refusing to give the dog back, then threatening to file a restraining order when he didn't leave me alone. I was only 23, but I was discovering my inner Mama Bear, the part of me that would fight to protect my charges at any cost.

For the next five years, I kept a picture of Zeke on my desk at school to remind me to focus not on punishing the worst in kids, but on bringing out their best. Zeke taught me how to use laughter and kindness to make my classroom a safe place for students, where they could grow into the best versions of themselves. The kids loved to hear stories about him, and instead of giving me the usual mugs and trinkets that teachers get, they gave me tennis balls and bones for Zeke. In class, we diagrammed sentences about him chasing squirrels and eating cheese. When they came back from the high school to visit me, they asked about him before anything else.

Zeke was a wonderful dog. I promised him I'd take care of him for as long as he lived, and when his time here was up, the vet came to our house and I lay on the floor with my head on the pillow of his dog bed, stroking his soft ears and whispering to him.

"You're a good dog," I told him. "You're my best dog." The whole family gathered around us, crying and petting him, but in the end it was just me and my best dog with our faces together, and I watched him close his eyes for the last time, knowing that he was perfectly safe and perfectly loved.

A few weeks after Zeke died, Trent Kidder graduated from high school. I heard that he grew up to be a serious, studious young man who argued passionately for his beliefs. I thought about him a lot during Zeke's last days. As a teacher, I often wished I could keep my students safe — as safe as I kept Zeke — for their entire lives. Still, a year is better than nothing, and I'm grateful to the dog who taught me to spend what little time I get with students teaching them that they are good people, that they are safe, and that they are loved.

M. Molly Backes lives in Chicago, writes for young adults, and stops to pet every dog she sees.

The Other Woman

Megan Sullivan

Supple and blond with limber legs and brown eyes capable of disarming even me, the jealous wife, Kiva is the quintessential other woman. On a recent Saturday night in Boston, my husband tried to articulate what Kiva means to him, and why, no matter how much he loves me, she will always be "his girl"—the other "woman" in our relationship.

"She taught me how to be the man I am today," my husband tells me before confiding that not only did he always feel confident when Kiva stood beside him, but also that he was flattered by the attention the two of them received. His confession makes me simultaneously raise one eyebrow and reconsider the term "eye candy." He senses my unease.

"Listen," he says, "the first time I went out alone without my cane, Kiva was there, guiding me around Boston with the confidence of a personal navigation system and the aplomb of the diva she is. The first time I rode the T alone at night without my white stick, Kiva was indispensible, side-stepping people and luggage and baby strollers." My husband pauses for a moment, not so much for effect, but to assess his feelings: "Kiva gave me my independence, and that's why she will always be my girl."

Carl and I met in 2003, so I did not know him when he flew to Michigan to greet Kiva, his first guide dog. I didn't know Carl when he found out he was going blind, or when he stopped driving and began adjusting to life as a visually impaired man. I was elsewhere in 1998

Kinley and Kiva

when he made the decision to ditch the white cane in favor of the beautiful yellow canine who would become his partner in independence. When we finally did meet, I was ignorant of the world one writer has astutely called "the planet of the blind," yet I was merely uninterested in another universe: the kingdom of dogs.

Picture this: a dark restaurant on a balmy summer night. A woman runs into a friend she hasn't seen all summer. She is introduced to the friend's handsome companion, and the three thirty-somethings talk. At some point the conversation turns to dogs. Because the restaurant is dark and the woman is taken with the man, and because she doesn't see the guide dog lying on the floor next to his chair, the woman speaks of a neighbor's dog as a "yappy mutt." There is an awkward pause, and the handsome man takes the opportunity to point out his guide dog. The woman backpedals: It's not that she dislikes dogs exactly, she clarifies, but rather that she never has the urge to kneel down in front of them or to stroke their ears. The woman refrains from further explanation, considering it unnecessary to parcel out that she has never had the desire to own a pet, to notice its hair bunched up in the corner of her stairway, or to shiver through a late night walk in the cold, January snow.

> "At our first kiss, Kiva jumps between us, assuming she too can play."

Despite the awkward events above, Carl begins to court me, and Kiva is omnipresent; not just guiding him along a street, but urging the two of us along in our relationship. On our first date, Kiva lies quiet and patient under the table as our "quick drink" morphs into appetizers, entrees, and desserts, and her seven o'clock walk is delayed until after ten. At our first kiss, Kiva jumps between us, assuming she too can play. Later, I watch out my window as Kiva bounds off the T with purposefulness and pride and guides Carl toward my apartment.

No one is more surprised than I am when I begin to fall for the dog as well as the man.

As my relationship with Carl progresses, I pay more attention to his relationship with Kiva. The two have an intuitive gait, to be sure, but it is more than that: they trust each other implicitly. As a unit, they move through streets and into stores and restaurants and workplaces. Carl signals "go right," and Kiva does so. Kiva pauses at a curb, sensing a car, and Carl stops. This is serious work they do, but they play well together too. Off harness: that is when Kiva is not working, Carl throws a ball, and Kiva fetches it. She lies down, and he scratches her belly. Kiva has had enough, and Carl backs off. They anticipate one another's needs and desires, and they know when to leave well enough alone.

Just before we got married, Kiva had knee surgery and retired. She still lives with us, but Carl also has a new guide dog, a black Labrador named Kinley. Kiva's retirement was hard at first—for all of us. On his way out the door to work, Carl would pick up the leash and harness, and Kiva would run toward it. "I'm sorry," I'd hear Carl whisper to Kiva from the other room, and I'd wipe the tears from my own eyes. We got through it, however; Kiva likes her new "brother" Kinley, and she loves her new dog walker. Now, Kiva bounces up to greet us at the end of the day, and Carl invariably says some form of the following: "How was my girl today? I can't wait to go out for a walk with you." That concern and desire seem a perfect thing for us all to aim for, and I'm glad the other woman taught me how to appreciate it.

Megan Sullivan is an Associate Professor of Rhetoric at Boston University. Although she does not usually write about dogs, her essay about Kiva might be a new beginning.

Coyote Pups

Chavawn Kelley

Perhaps it's because Wyoming is the least populated state in the country that we all have dogs. Every yard has a dog. Every truck. Every ranch. Every signpost and bike rack in front of every small-town café has a leash tied around it, a dog patiently waiting at the end of it. Aussies, Healers and Border Collies. Labradors and Golden Retrievers. Can any adult or free-roaming child claim citizenship here without the association of his or her dedicated four-legged flesh?

As long as my husband and I were merely renting, I could resist the pull, but once we bought a house with an enclosed yard, I lost the will to remain dogless. I yearned to join the dominant culture. I wanted a beautiful dog, alert, agile and calm. A friendly dog, a watchdog—one that would not dig holes.

As if we walked into a divine setup, Shaun and I found Sasha on a mountaintop. We hiked the rugged trail to the summit of Medicine Bow Peak, and there in the boulders, out of the wind, sat two women with two dogs. One dog with each, I assumed, but I was wrong; both belonged to one owner. Sasha was like no dog I had ever seen. Long fur in shades of red and gold with an undercoat of butter cream. A Border Collie-Husky mix, they guessed. And, as fate would have it, Sasha needed a home.

On the way down, the canines ran in unleashed glory over rock and trail through autumn grass. They leapt into the wild, unconcerned

Sasha

with us. The warmth of the day gave way to the cool of late afternoon, and by the time we reached Mirror Lake, Shaun and I had received the offer of a dog.

By most measures, this was not a good time. We were to adopt a baby and become parents in less than eight weeks. It did not bode well that Sasha had been given up by a young couple upon the recent birth of *their* first child. But if our lives were going to change with the call from the adoption agency, telling us, "Come now," why couldn't we prepare by bringing home a dog?

I cannot say that Sasha bonded with us immediately. She adjusted. She endured the menacing stares of our cats. We did not change her name but added "Belle" to register our affection. Sasha Belle. We noted her propensity for chasing small animals and nipping at bicycles.

Three weeks before Joseph was born, Sasha was attacked by an English Bulldog named Diesel. The puncture wound penetrated her abdomen completely. Her breathing became labored, her pulse thready. As Shaun and I stood by the stainless steel surgical table, I knew as well as any nonparent could that this was what it felt like to fear for your child. No longer were we strangers or acquaintances. Sasha was our dog now, and we belonged to her. A change had taken place. The pink of her shaved skin and scars disappeared into the growth of fur, and by the time Joseph arrived, there could be no doubt about the makeup of our family.

When we got Sasha, no one said, "Oh, I didn't know you wanted a dog." Yet it was a surprise to many when we became parents, and in the clamor of well wishes, that was the only comment that stung. "Oh, I didn't know you wanted a child." What did they expect? That we would air our failure or betray our grief?

Last summer, returning from a camping trip in the Big Horn Mountains, we traveled through the Shirley Basin, south of Casper. The land is expansive, with limestone hills and sparse vegetation. The standard route is desolate, but on this trip, Shaun took the old highway, which is both desolate and neglected, relegated mostly to ranch access. The road pitched us up swales and elicited "Whee!" on the way down. From the seat in the back, Joseph, now a toddler, informed us he had to go. There is nowhere to stop on Highway 77. Or you can stop anywhere you like, depending on your view of things. We turned off onto a dirt road and pulled over.

"Okay Joseph," we told him after he further explained his situation, "poop like a coyote." At coyote level, you could see the hoof prints where cows had ranged, their manure piles weathered to the gray of the dirt. Rocks you could fit in your pocket were scattered across the basin floor like failed monuments. Sasha nosed about, sensing an alternate universe. She wetted the earth. "Poop like a coyote," we entreated. We'd seen their scat on the boulders in the Big Horns and heard their calls at dusk. In Shirley Basin in the colorless light of mid afternoon, Joseph crouched and considered and finally complied. Our little coyote. We collected the prize.

"How old is Sasha?" our neighbor asked, recently.

I told her Sasha was about a year and a half old when we got her, so she must be about six.

"Where we used to live there was a dog that looked exactly like her a couple of houses down," she said. "She was kept tied up and didn't get enough to eat."

Of course it could have been another dog from the same litter, but our neighbor was certain it was Sasha.

"That dog was half Border Collie and half coyote," she said.

Sasha a coyote? I couldn't get the thought out of my head. For days, I re-imagined her with this new knowledge.

"Are you a coyote?" I asked.

> "I knew as well as any non-parent could that this was what it felt like to fear for your child."

Her ears perked, she looked up with those maple eyes, her tail beat the floor. Yes! It is always a good time for a walk! I studied the shape of her. I watched her run in the field. I recalled the time she got loose and killed two chickens. The time she killed a squirrel mid-air. I considered calling a zoologist I knew who was conducting a coyote study. Maybe she could tell me something.

There is a lot we don't know about our son. Mother and father filled out information sheets with ancestry and medical history. I remember before he was born, his young mother said something about an incident. The father was angry about her decision and confronted her. The upset affected the baby, and the next day she had to go to the doctor.

Why didn't I listen more carefully when she told me this? I don't know. But what difference would it have made? And she smoked. But again, what difference does that make now?

Sasha has freckles on her muzzle like a Border Collie and stripes from her eyes to her ears like a Husky. She pulls hard like Husky, herds like a Border Collie. If anyone asks, I don't say she's part coyote. She is all Sasha.

Chavawn Kelley has received writing fellowships from the Wyoming Arts Council, the Ucross Foundation and Can Serrat International Arts Center (Spain). Her work has been published in *Creative Nonfiction*, *Quarterly West*, *Hayden's Ferry Review*, and other journals, and has been nominated for the Pushcart Prize and cited in *Best American Essays*. She lives in Laramie, Wyoming.

Kismet

Julie Fredrick

Kismet: (noun) Fate; a predetermined or unavoidable destiny.

I had just visited the fourth pet rescue group of the day, and my hope was growing dim. Of all the wonderful dogs I'd seen in the past two months, none met all of the qualifications I had listed in my mind. She would be my "golden girl," a Golden Retriever mix (though I would consider Yellow Lab or Setter mixes), and she'd be six months or younger. She had to be out there.

Three months prior, my heart was ripped from my chest, leaving an abyss that threatened to swallow me alive. My husband Jeff and I had gone to the beach to visit my parents and entrusted our two precious dogs to Ed, a friend of Jeff's, who promised to care for them as he would his own. On the third day of our trip, Jeff received a phone call. It was Ed.

"Hey, Jeff, listen, man, I can't seem to find your dogs. They took off."

I knew from the alarm in Jeff's voice that this was not just a friendly chat. It turned out that Ed had had a party with fireworks and left our dogs outside. Now, sixteen hours later, they were nowhere to be found.

Panic ensued as we called the airline and arranged for the next available flight home. Every possible scenario played in my head. *Are they OK? Are they together? Quiche is terrified of fireworks.* I prayed they hadn't gone near the highway. Our dogs were our babies, our family.

Kismet

We planned our life around them, and included them in nearly every event. I felt the terror of a mother whose child has failed to get off the school bus.

We arrived home that evening and began the desperate search. At 2 A.M., we agreed to try to sleep and resume our search at first light. By six the next morning, Jeff was scouring the roads to our north, while I placed "Lost Dogs" signs in the surrounding neighborhoods and parks.

Just before noon, I heard our Jeep pull into the driveway. I held my breath and waited for Jeff to enter. The look on his face needed no explanation. He stepped toward me just as I hit the floor screaming, "NO! No no no no!"

"I'm so sorry! Oh, God, I'm so sorry!" Jeff fell to his knees trying, unsuccessfully, to hold me. He found Sophie and Quiche on the side of the road, together, looking as peaceful as if they had just lain down for a nap. They had both been hit. He picked up their lifeless bodies and placed them in the Jeep and drove home. I forced myself off the floor and went outside to see them. I put my face to each of their necks and stroked behind their ears, as I had done every day of their lives.

Our world was turned upside down. These were our only children. I had rescued Sophie, a scruffy Spaniel mix, from an animal shelter ten years before. Quiche, a Golden Retriever mix, had adopted us eight years before this tragedy, when he showed up on our doorstep with a too-tight piece of rope around his neck, afraid of his own shadow.

Now they were gone. Jeff took a week off work to stay at home with me, and my parents rushed to be by my side, but I was inconsolable. Eventually, Jeff returned to work and my parents returned to Florida. The silence in our house was deafening. I found it difficult to get out of bed. I wasn't working at the time, and Jeff was required to travel out of town, so there wasn't much incentive to do anything. On the rare occasion when I did go out, the prospect of returning to an empty home lured me deeper into the chasm that engulfed my soul.

The symptoms of depression that I had battled most of my life returned with a vengeance. My appetite was gone, sleep fluctuated between fit-ful and constant, and I cried throughout the day and night. Days passed when I realized that I had not spoken a word. I relied on alco-hol to mask the pain and began smoking again. I lost all interest in my appearance and personal hygiene. Jeff's concern mounted. "Let's get together with some friends this weekend," he'd say, or, "Your parents would love for you to visit them." But my apathy overruled everything.

After two months and countless discussions with Jeff, I began to toy with the idea of getting another dog. Conflicting dialog ran through my head, both teasing me with possibilities and highlighting my doubts. *Am I ready to open my heart? How could I possibly love another dog?* I had to do something to pull myself out of this hole.

So my search began. I frequented animal shelters and humane soci-
eties, but I couldn't find that "you'll know her when you see her" dog.
I had it all worked out in my mind. I envisioned a female version of
Quiche (getting a female made her seem like less of an attempt at total
replacement). She would love swimming in the lake beside our house,
going on fast runs and long hikes alongside Jeff and me, and curling
up at our feet at the end of a complete day.

Just as I was leaving the last adoption site at the end of another fruitless
search, a large woman with untamed gray hair and knowing eyes
approached me. I had noticed her watching me as I made my way
between the kennels of canines waiting for a home.

"Are you okay, honey?"

"Oh, I'm fine, just sorta looking, you know."

"You seem sad. I think I have someone that you need to meet, but he's
not here." Then she showed me a blurry picture of a small, grey Benji-
looking dog."It's cute," I said, "but…" I proceeded to describe my
ideal companion. The woman replied, "He's special, this one is. He's
been with me for over a year, and I won't let him go until I find his
'perfect person.' There's something about you. I think you need to
meet him." She gave me her phone number and told me to think
about him. I stuck the scrap of paper in my pocket. As I left, I turned
back to her.

"What's his name?"

"Kismet."

When I got home, Jeff asked me how my search that day had gone.
"Nothing," I replied, as I had on so many previous occasions. That
night I slept little. The next morning, I fished through my pockets in
search of the phone number the woman had given me. I picked up the
phone and punched in the numbers with trepidation.

"Hi. I met you yesterday. I'm calling about Kismet."

"Hi, honey. This is Sherry. I had a feeling you might call. Would you like to come meet him?"

Jeff and I drove out to the country and were at Sherry's house in an hour. I was nervous and reminded Jeff that we were just going to take a look. I needed to know why this dog had invaded my thoughts all night, especially since he bore no similarities to the dog I had in mind. Sherry carried Kismet out of the house and set him down in the yard. He was rambunctious and obviously happy to be out of his cage. He ran in circles and barked unabashedly. His long grey coat flowed behind him as he darted from tree to tree. I observed him closely. He was small, maybe 20 pounds, just over a year old. Definitely a terrier of some sort, with a voice like a freight train more suited to a giant breed. He was as far removed from a Golden Retriever as you could get. He greeted me with jumps and licks, and lay in my lap, contented, the whole way home.

> "Am I ready to open my heart? How could I possibly love another dog?"

During Kismet's first few days with us, my apprehension kept me from allowing myself to love him unconditionally. I studied him with reserve, scrutinizing his actions.

"Maybe we should change his name," I announced one morning. "He's kinda goofy—maybe something like Gizmo, or Taz or something."

"Let's just get to know him better," responded the always-sensible Jeff.

When the dog lifted his leg and marked the couch, I found myself second-guessing my decision to adopt the little foreigner. Even though Quiche had done just that on the very same couch when he was a puppy, I had buried any memories that might render him just an ordinary dog, doing what dogs do. Kismet also barked, a lot. He barked when anyone came to the door, including Jeff and me. Jeff gently reminded me that just a week ago it was the silence in our house that made me feel so empty.

As the days passed and my life began to regain some sense of routine, Kismet steadily became part of our lives. I once again had a reason to get out of bed in the morning. As soon as Jeff let him out of the kitchen, where Kismet slept in an open crate, he bounded into the bedroom and leapt on the bed, demanding my attention. Try as I might to be cranky at having my face licked so early, I loved feeling the puppy love that washed over me.

Kismet's independent nature stood out when I took him to the park and tried to teach him to retrieve a tennis ball, as Quiche and Sophie had so loved to do. He was indifferent to chasing, much less bringing back, anything that I threw for him. He was more interested in the abundant squirrels and other dogs that walked within sight. *He just doesn't want to play with me*, I thought.

"He sure has a mind of his own," Jeff observed. *Just like me*, I mused.

I resumed taking walks around the neighborhood, with Kismet pulling on his leash in an attempt to smell everything within reach. His boundless energy and enthusiasm for life was strong encouragement for me to begin running again, and I found myself laughing aloud as he wagged his entire body rowdily while I fastened his leash.

"Are you ready, Little Man? Wanna run with Mommy?" He answered me with licks. *I've been ready all my life!* It was good to get out again, after having quit any form of exercise for the previous several months. Eventually our evening exercise replaced my need to sit with my depression, cigarette and drink in hand.

One evening, as Kismet and I sat together on the front porch, I realized that I was staring intently at my dog without a glimmer of doubt. He was so different from any dog I had ever met, in both looks and personality. Yet those very differences nearly kept me from ever letting him into my heart. I realized that sometimes it's best to let go of our preconceptions and stop trying so hard to influence how our lives will play out.

In due course, I began to crawl out of the void within. Slowly. One hand at a time, I grasped the edge and hauled myself up. Once my head was high enough to look around, I realized that life had continued to happen. And I was ready to join in again. After all, Kismet was waiting.

Julie Fredrick lives in Atlanta, Georgia with her husband and two rescued dogs. She volunteers with refugees and visits nursing homes with Roxie, a Border Collie mix. She is an avid traveler and is currently writing a collection of stories about her experiences and misadventures.

Our Four-Legged Antidote

Francine L. Billingslea

Mom and I were out doing our Saturday shopping and running errands when she suddenly suggested we stop by the pet adoption center and check out the dogs. Not really interested, but willing to humor her, I agreed. "Okay, but remember, we're just looking," I said. "No adopting!"

Mom always had a love for dogs and we had been talking about getting one. I knew a dog would be good company for both of us and I wanted one just as much as she did. However, since we were always on the go, I felt that getting a dog at this particular time would be a hindrance.

As we walked up and down the aisles of caged, barking dogs, I was secretly thankful that they were all large, scary and unattractive—the complete opposite of what we had in mind. Walking ahead of my mother, I looked back and saw that she was slowly and carefully examining each dog with a disappointed look. Reaching the door that led out to the office, I stood and waited for her, feeling bad that she did not see a dog she liked.

At the front desk, I asked the receptionist for the location of the next closest adoption center. As she printed out the directions, the door opened and in walked a young woman struggling to hold onto a cute, wiggling little puppy. The dog suddenly leaped out of her arms and my mother caught him, hugging and cradling him as if he were a baby. As

Max

he barked and licked my mother's face, she laughed and giggled with approval. I'll always remember how my mother's face lit up. It was love at first sight.

The owner had tears in her eyes as she told us that her husband was in the military and they were moving and could not bring Max. My mother, who was still holding onto him, yelled like an excited child, "We'll take him!" I quickly and silently agreed. We walked out to the owner's car and she gave us his food, cage, bowl, extra leashes, toys, his papers showing that he was a six month-old neutered male Poodle/Schnauzer mix. His tail was clipped, his ears cropped and his coat boasted soft grayish-tan curls, with sprays of straight black hairs pointing through. He was small, medium built and oh, so handsome. We paid the small fee, thanked and hugged the previous owner, and put Max into the back of our SUV. He never once looked back as I drove the newest member of our family to his new home. That night I gave Max a warm bath and we all settled in, happy and contented. A few days later, I took him to the pet shop for grooming and a thorough exam. The vet said he was a strong, healthy, happy puppy. We had hit the doggie jackpot!

Max was comfortably incorporated into our family and into our lives. How had we gotten along without him? He became my mother's best friend, and I quickly saw how therapeutic Max was for her. I enjoyed watching them play and run around the yard like two kids. Even though Mom stayed busy with her senior group, Max made a significant difference in her life and attitude.

It was definitely better than anything the doctor could have ordered. She spoiled him by taking him for a ride every day, which has since become an imperative part of his daily routine. It is essential to put the windows half way down, allowing him enough room to stand and stick his upper body out. As the wind blows his long mustache back, he looks as if he's smiling as he barks his hellos, threats and whatever else. Satisfied with his ride, he comes home, lies on his back, paws bent in the air, and takes a short nap.

> "Max was trying to tell me he was there for me, that he loved me and it was going to be alright."

A year after we welcomed Max into our family, my mother very suddenly passed and Max grieved right along with the rest of us. We would call and look for him, only to find him lying under her bed, sad. You could clearly see that he missed her. For a while, he even carried one of Mom's socks around between his teeth. I realized that dogs have feelings too, possibly not so different from our own.

Shortly after mom's death, I was diagnosed with breast cancer, and Max, sensing that something was wrong with me, became overly protective and more company than I could ever have imagined. He almost never let me out of his sight. He would lie beside me and lick my face or my hairless head, as if he were trying to tell me he was there for me, that he loved me and it was going to be alright.

It also seemed as though he became more patient. If I was sleeping and his food bowl was empty or he needed to go outside, he waited without protest. My daughter and her fiancé had keys to the house, and when they came over, he would greet them at the door and lead them to whatever room I was in. Then he'd lie right there watching every move they made. Once they left, he'd jump in the bed or on the couch and cuddle up to me.

During this time, I was seldom left alone and if I was, it wasn't for long. One day, my daughter came over to pick up a list of things I needed from the store. She was gone only a few minutes when she called to ask me something and got no answer. Another few calls yielded first no answer, then busy signals. Concerned that I was having some kind of problem, she left the store and hurried to my home. Max greeted her excitedly and led her to where I was: the floor. I had passed out and was too hurt and weak to get to the phone. In trying to help in his own way, Max had knocked the phone off the receiver, thereby sending out the busy signal that brought help to me.

We all think that our dogs are special, but I don't just think this: I *know* mine is. He offered me comfort, love and companionship when I was ill. It is because of him that I stay true to my daily exercise of walking and because of him that I have made quite a few friends, especially at the park. He makes me laugh, and it gives me a good feeling having him around, especially when I'm missing my mother or feeling the "empty nest syndrome."

I believe that if you take proper care of your dog and give it love, that love will be returned. I also believe that if you or any member of the family is in any kind of danger, it will instinctively do anything it can to save or help you and will even put its life on the line for you. Dogs are much smarter than we think and are sometimes greatly underestimated. I know that's how it is with Max; he's proven that to me. There's something special about having a sincere love in your life. Of course, nothing can top the love of another human being, but the love and the benefits that you give and receive from having a dog has got to be second on the list. He's my shining sun on a stormy day.

Francine L. Billingslea is a retired member of the United Auto Workers union, breast cancer survivor, proud mother of one and grandmother to four, who is currently pursuing a newly found passion for writing. She spends her retirement traveling, spending time with her loved ones and with her best friend, Max. She is currently writing her autobiography, focusing on her victory over breast cancer.

On Laughter

Bobbi Arduini

Laughter was raised along interstate on-ramps, behind fast food restaurants, and in national forests. We were hitchhikers, and he spent most of his puppyhood tied to a belt loop on my patchwork jeans.

Laughter and I had a routine for life on the road. We started out each morning waking up beneath an overpass. I rolled up my sleeping bad and shoved it into my backpack, and then we walked to the nearest gas station. At the gas station, I tied Laughter's leash to the pack and ran inside to brush my teeth, scrounge up some change for coffee, and fill up a large plastic bowl with tap water. Before heading out to the on-ramp, Laughter and I had our playtime. He didn't have any toys, so I balled a sock up tight, and we played keep away.

When ready to face the long day of hitching, Laughter and I walked to the on-ramp and planted ourselves in plain view, which also tended to be in direct sunlight. The back of my neck blistered and burned and scabbed as Laughter panted, trying to sneak away from me, heading for the shady growth of scraggly interstate trees about twenty feet back. We sat there for hours some mornings. I smiled and stuck my thumb out at every car, flashing peace signs as they drove past. Sometimes, if we were desperate, I drew attention to us by picking up Laughter and dancing with him by the side of the road, performing mock waltzes or disco moves. Laughter's four little legs would dangle in the air and his ears, which hadn't straightened yet, would flop in the breeze, and we'd

Laughter

spin around, my face stretched into a silly smile, Laughter's sharp puppy teeth reaching for my nose.

Laughter never saw me dope sick, wanting to scratch my own skin off because it hurt so much trying to kick heroin and crack. He missed that by a week. We'd met in New Mexico, in the high desert outside Taos. I had recently left New Orleans, hopped into a VW bus and driven for three days with some new friends to go on some spiritual camping retreat. The details were a blur. It seemed to me as if one day I'd been playing darts with my crack dealers, and the next day I was in the woods, sitting around a campfire with someone called Gypsy Moon Mama.

I wanted to go back home, which at that time meant my ex-boyfriend's cockroach-infested apartment with no electricity or running water, because at least I understood that world. I took a walk by myself, hiking to the top of this cliff where there were other people camping. I was scared and lonely and so I decided, or felt, that something was waiting for me at the top of that cliff, that something was promised to me so long as I didn't stop for a cigarette or pause to catch my breath. It was early morning and it was cold; sunlight filtered through the pine trees in soft yellow patterns, clouds formed in the distance. When I reached the top of the rise, I buckled over, panting for breath.

An old man with blue eyes walked over to me from one of the camp-fires. He asked if I wanted a puppy. And then there was this little brown wriggling thing in my arms. I looked down into golden eyes and the puppy looked up into mine—it whined and cried—and I started crying, too. I named him Laughter and told that old man that this was a lucky pup, that he was going to a good home.

A good home is not a crack house, but I was afraid if I stayed in one place too long, I might start using hard drugs again. So for the first year of Laughter's life, we were hitchhikers. I started off trying to train Laughter, trying to be a good master. I could eat out of dumpster, that was fine for me, but only the best dry dog food was good enough for my puppy. Since good dog food runs at least thirteen bucks a bag, Laughter and I had to make money. We didn't work especially hard – mostly just sat outside grocery stores with a cardboard sign that read *Trying to get home. Will work for dog food.* I did the talking; Laughter looked cute. People had a lot of questions for us: Where was home? Where the heart is. Why were we homeless? I preferred the term "houseless." When people raised their eyebrows at his ribs and bony hips, I explained about his fast metabolism. Besides, I argued, most of America's dogs are grossly obese. Laughter wasn't skinny; he was trim and lean. Laughter wagged his tail and gratefully accepted all handouts—from dog bones to steak, the latter of which he shared with me. I might have made light of it occasionally when challenged by people who were concerned about

Laughter's health, but I always put his well-being first. Nothing was more important to me than the health of my puppy.

Then, after many hours alongside lonely highways, I began to believe in Laughter as something more than a dog. He became my guide. I believed that he'd been sent to me as a kind of cosmic gift to help me learn how to be a good person. Nothing Laughter did went unanalyzed. I believed that his actions paralleled mine. If Laughter was itchy, it was time for me to wash myself. If Laughter stumbled, it was symbolic of my own actions. Worst of all, if Laughter got sick, there was something terribly wrong with me.

> "I looked down into golden eyes and the puppy looked up into mine—it whined and cried—and I started crying, too."

We lived like that for months, and Laughter was sick quite often. Vet care was hard to come by. I tried natural remedies that I learned from other hitchhikers. For fleas, feed him garlic. For tapeworms, feed him small bits of tobacco. None of these, however, were effective. At the end of the year, Laughter had fleas and I had lice. We were both sick and confused and I had no idea what to do about it. As a last resort, I called my parents in New York. And then everything changed for us. We moved back into my mom's house. Laughter was taken to the vet, given shots and antibiotics. I, after a shower and good scrub with Nix, was taken to the psychologist. Laughter got "fixed" and I was enrolled in college.

The move home was not a smooth transition for either of us. We'd been on the streets for a year; there were practical problems. Never having been in a house for longer than a day, Laughter had never been house-trained. He was perfectly car-trained, I argued in his defense, but when my mom pointed to the fresh pile of waste under the pool table, all I could do was shrug and grab the vinegar, paper towels and air freshener.

I, on the other hand, felt that I had lost my usefulness. I knew how to be homeless; I was good at it. I knew how to find the best food in the grocery store dumpster, how to talk to a trucker for over 500 miles without letting the ride get dangerous or boring. On the other hand, I didn't know how to stand in line at the Registrar's office, or how to gracefully use a grocery cart.

Laughter and I spent a lot of time together, but I started noticing some changes in him. On the road he had become a kind of sage, but the longer my mom fed him ground beef for dinner, and the more my brother made him shake paw, the more *dog-like* he became. He picked up bizarre behaviors—chasing his tail, mooching at the dinner table, constantly squeaking his new toys. My psychologist told me this was natural, that Laughter had never gotten to be a real puppy and it was now his turn to live the life he'd missed out on. Or maybe she never told me that at all. Maybe that's what I told her while she nodded and again asked me about my drug use.

When I transferred from the community college to a four-year school, the hardest part was leaving Laughter behind in my mother's care. I didn't trust her with him. She was afraid to walk him; Laughter had grown to 75 pounds and had become aggressive toward other dogs. He'd taken to sitting on the arm of the couch, staring out the window like an overgrown cat. If another dog walked by, Laughter slammed himself into the glass, barking and snarling at the offending dog. He was quickly becoming a neighborhood legend: the mean dog in the window.

If she was afraid to walk him, though, she wasn't afraid to feed him. Laughter enjoyed meals of chicken soup, tuna fish, buttered toast, and cube steak. With every visit home, I noticed Laughter's rounding belly. When I complained, my mom shrugged and said he wouldn't eat dry kibble anymore. He'd wait, the poor thing, until he was given something he liked.

I visited home often, staying for long weekends. I didn't like being in college. I missed Laughter and I hated living in a dorm. I was constantly in trouble with the housing department for breaking the rules—camping in the quad, inviting homeless people into the dorms, painting murals on college property. I worried that Laughter would forget about our time on the road. Every time I came home I took him aside, looked into his eyes and promised that as soon as I got my degree, we'd return to our old life, our simple life, when all we had to worry about was finding a safe place to sleep and raising enough spare change for a bag of Iams. At hearing this, Laughter licked my face and then struggled out of my arms. Mom was cooking ground beef in the kitchen and he didn't want to miss out.

Laughter and I never did hitchhike together again. By the time I finished my years at college, my priorities had shifted. It was time for graduate school, and this time Laughter was coming with me. When I moved from New York to California, Laughter rode shotgun for three thousand miles. I realized with new clarity how unfair that kind of life would be for him. Maybe as a puppy the car had seemed like a vast space full of hiding spots and curiosities. For Laughter the full-grown dog, though, it was hot and cramped. Every two hundred miles or so he'd start to whine: Are we at the next gas station yet?

When we got to Oakland, we discovered something else: dog parks. Laughter, with his tendency toward fighting, wasn't safe to run off-leash unless muzzled. I never thought I could put a muzzle on him, but now, to see him wading into the small waves of the Bay is amazing. He's never had it so good. Other dog owners take in the muzzle and my alert eyes. They pull me aside every so often, and recommend good dog psychologists, good dog trainers. One woman with long silver hair held my hand gently and smiled. "He's got to learn how to play," she said, "then he'll calm down." I smiled back at her, thinking that I finally fit in somewhere.

We've been in the Bay Area for a little while. Sometimes I think I see progress. Laughter is properly housetrained. I'm still clumsy with the grocery cart and I still need people to remind me sometimes that life is better now. But when I watch Laughter chase his tail and shake paw and bark at poodles I can see myself in my dog. He's just like me, I think. A slow learner.

Bobbi Arduini and Laughter live in Oakland, California. Bobbi received a Masters degree in Fine Arts in Creative Nonfiction from Saint Mary's College. She now teaches high school English.

Winston's Boy

Lisa Preston

By late December in Anchorage, Alaska, the streets are sheeted in bumpy ice with crusts of snow mounding at the road shoulders. It made for tricky and tiring driving, especially for someone like me who worked the night shift. Driving home on a day nearing the winter solstice, I was eager to fall asleep, glad to be almost home. Then, just before turning off the main road to drive the last few blocks home, I saw the body.

The little dog was lying at the edge of the street and appeared undamaged except for the smallest bit of dried blood on his nose. Although he was obviously dead his soft body still gave to my touch. Undoubtedly, he'd been hit by a car and, here at the roadside, his life had ended.

His coat was a lovely cinnamon, with thick, rich fur that suggested a Chow lineage. I checked the tag on his collar and learned that "Winston" had only been a couple of blocks from home when he died. He was small enough that I could have picked him up, but something made me hesitate and instead I left him there and drove alone to the address inscribed on the tag.

The front yard of the house had sleds and balls and assorted bright plastic toys. I walked past these things with my head bent low, holding my breath as I knocked. When no young faces came to the door, I sighed with relief. No adults came to the door either, so I thought

Jack

about leaving a note. Again I hesitated, not knowing what to write. How could I write a note that would inform the parents what had happened without telling the children?

Winston's tag had the phone number on it as well, so in the end, I simply left a message on the owners' phone machine, giving my name and number, asking that they call me about their dog. Before going to bed, I called the animal shelter and asked that they pick up the body.

The sad situation was gone from my mind as I awoke and went back to work, but when I came home again, there were messages waiting on the answering machine. A young boy had called over and over, wanting to know if I had a dog.

Yes, I had a dog. Jack was a large, strikingly beautiful Golden Retriever, feathered in every shade of yellow from the palest silvery gild to a honey burnished as red as Winston's coat. With the dawning realization that the family must have called the shelter, I felt my stomach lurch. Suppose the boy thought that I was the one who had killed his dog? I called him back with reluctance, dreading talk of his loss, hesitant to hear his sorrow.

> "With tears on his cheeks, the boy helped Jack pull the paper off each gift and inspect them one by one."

His voice sounded as shaky as I felt. "I was wondering, if you have a dog," he asked immediately. I told him I did, not understanding why he wanted to know, wondering if he'd soon be asking how I'd feel if I lost my dog right before Christmas. I still didn't know if he thought I was the one who killed his pet.

"So… I wanted to know if I could give Winston's Christmas presents…" the boy's voice broke but he recovered and managed to finish, "…to your dog."

Jack and I went over right away. The boy was older than I thought he'd be, maybe ten or eleven, and he was home alone. With the friendly enthusiasm typical of his breed, Jack went right up and plunged his face into the large grocery bag the boy was holding. Wrapped present after wrapped present came up, clasped gently in Jack's jaws. Dog treats, a rawhide chew toy, a ball. With tears on his cheeks, the boy helped Jack pull the paper off each gift and inspect them one by one.

I don't know if the boy told me his name. I couldn't have remembered, could hardly trust my voice not to crack when I thanked him and drove Jack home with his new belongings. That boy's profound sense of Christmas, wanting to give gifts in his grief, was an experience to keep in my heart forever. And so, while it was a brief encounter and I was sad for his loss, I'll always treasure that time I had with Winston's boy.

Lisa Preston is a Northwest writer whose work includes non-fiction about dogs and horses.

Lola Bean Pod

Kim Lute

Let me tell you about a dog I know. Her name is Lola Bean Pod. She's the dog you find yourself staring at, and not because she is wearing a sweater that resembles your own. She is special because she's full of soul, a virtual cyclone of loyalty, emotion and unabashed honesty. Maya Angelou wrote, "A great soul serves everyone all the time." And while Lola Bean's ceremonious stride and sometimes crotchety demeanor might suggest otherwise, the true measure of her fidelity was never more obvious than during the summer of 2007.

When my liver started to fail that August and I lost my appetite, Lola Bean also lost her appetite. I stayed in bed for days and she remained underneath it, lethargic but mindful of my every toss and turn, letting out an occasional growl when she wanted to remind me that she stood sentry. When I was able to move around, she kept pace with me, paused when I needed to catch my breath and resumed her distinctive trot when I was ready to continue on. Lola Bean kept me engaged and aware at a time when my body began to falter, when the jaundice turned my eyes and complexion a cautionary shade of yellow.

Some people say we look alike. Our personalities (for better or worse) are similar, and I often look down to see her looking up at me with a similar bewildered countenance. I'm partly to blame for her lack of patience and her tendency to place herself at the center of everyone's universe. No one, however, can take credit for her ability to create last-

Lola Bean Pod

ing impressions—chock full of comic asides—that makes it harder for other dogs hoping to capture your heart.

The day my fiancé Marcus and I first spotted her at a pet store in Atlanta, all the other dogs had their noses pressed against the cages except for Lola Bean, who kept her back to everyone. When I tapped on the glass, she looked over her shoulder with thinly-veiled disinterest. I turned to Marcus and said, "That's the one I want."

She had flaxen hair and an adorable tendency to furl herself into a ball before pitching herself forward at alarming speeds. Lola Bean, as we later learned, deals only in the extremes. She is at times both moody and deliriously happy. She either has one protective paw on your arm, or she's clearly defining *her* space, claiming *her* toys, and pointing out the apparent boundaries *you've* crossed. Lola Bean was considering us as companions as much as we were considering her as a pet. She curled against our ankles, then retreated to a corner. Were we suitable parents? Could we match her boundless energy? This gimlet-eyed Silky Terrier studied our every move. It took Lola Bean only minutes to deem us worthy. She lurched toward us with a genuine acceptance that seemed to scream, "You'll do just fine!"

Marcus and I do not have children, so she became our baby. She became such a large part of our lives that we could hardly remember a time when she wasn't. We ate when she ate. We slept when she slept. Our schedules complimented her play dates, her veterinary appointments and her frequent trips to the salon.

As my liver rejection advanced, Lola Bean's days became less structured, scattered even. She continued to stay close by, moving only as far as the hallway off the bedroom; although I suspect that her imagination took her farther away. I would sit in bed listening to her playing alone, barking at nothing in particular and tossing balls and random socks into the air until the joy of it all left her in need of a nap. Lola Bean, who we thought needed constant stimulation, including background classical music (specifically Antonin Dvorak) and a hoard of diverting toys (generally Disney characters), was fine on her own.

However, even the most resilient face grueling challenges when illness strikes, then lingers. When I was fifteen, I was diagnosed with chronic hepatitis and subsequently underwent a liver transplant when I turned twenty-two. Two years later, I lost my large intestine after being diagnosed with ulcerative colitis, another disease of the immune system. Doctors at University Hospital in my hometown of Denver, Colorado, worked tirelessly to create a future for me where none seemed to exist. Three years later, after I had moved to Atlanta to work as a journalist, I learned I had primary sclerosing cholangitis, a liver disease that caused me to have a second transplant. That was in 2001. I will always have to take medicine to suppress an immune system bent on attacking an organ it refuses to recognize as its own. The possibility of liver rejection is one of the few certainties in what has become an otherwise uncertain life.

That summer of 2007, my liver enzymes soared and my body again turned against itself. Highly-touted immunosuppressant drugs failed to help. I could hardly see beyond my own anxieties and limitations. Could my new doctors in Atlanta get a handle on the rejection? Would I ever get out of the bed I was practically tethered to? The worst of it came on the morning doctors told me I'd lapsed into a "temporary" diabetic state due to the high dosage of steroids I was taking. Sure, it was a manageable setback, but it was a setback nonetheless. As they detailed the many times a day I needed to test my blood sugar and where I should give myself insulin shots, I sank to the floor, my head in my hands. At some point I wandered toward an upstairs bathroom and closed myself inside it, losing track of my one constant: Lola Bean.

> "Maybe she knew all along that I'd be okay if I drew from her optimism."

As it happened, she had followed me up and was waiting outside the door. When I finally got hold of myself, I heard her pacing back and forth outside. Then, suddenly, I heard a thump against the door. To appease her, I wiggled my fingers under the crack, but this was a paltry attempt at reassurance. The thumping continued. I was shocked when I later realized that she had collected all of her toys and then tossed them at the door. As soon as I opened the door, she eyed me suspiciously before taking a toy in her mouth and shaking it furiously. When this failed to cheer me up, she flipped onto her back, kicked her paws into the air and let out a series of playful yelps. I smiled, hoping to appease her, but Lola Bean's always had impossibly high standards. She sprinted around the room a few of times before landing at my feet with an expression that demanded I pick her up. I gathered her in my arms and she began to kiss me until I was laughing through tears.

From then on, each time the phone rang she acted preemptively, dashing off to collect toys she then piled at my feet. Perhaps jostling with her and her toys was the antidote I'd needed all along. I certainly felt better when presented with every one of her stuffed animals. Or maybe she knew all along that I'd be okay if I drew from her optimism.

By summer's end, the rejection began to reverse and the wonder drugs finally proved wondrous. The diabetic state abated as the steroid dosage was lowered. Liver biopsies and twice-weekly blood draws became less frequent, and Lola Bean and I started to gain weight. She spent less time under the bed, less time lifting my spirits, and more time outdoors charming our neighbors in her pink fuzzy sweaters. We could hardly keep up as her social calendar blossomed. Our family was once again operating at a fever pitch. And there was no one more adamant that we relish the moment than Lola Bean Pod whose confidence seemed to scream, "We'll be just fine!"

Kim Lute is a DuPont and Peabody Award-winning journalist at CNN. Recently her reports have appeared in newspapers in Sweden and Denmark, and The University of Denver Magazine has published one of her autobiographical essays. Her most important job, however, is caring for Lola Bean Pod.

Silky

Gail Dudley

The little black dog had been hit by a car on Grand Avenue. Alive and still moving, she lay on the garbage-strewn shoulder of the road. An animal control officer was dispatched to pick her up after a rush-hour commuter dialed 911 from his cell phone.

When she arrived at the Maricopa County pound, she was taken immediately to the clinic. Just a puppy, barely six months old, she weighed only eight pounds. Her X-rays showed no broken bones, but there were signs of internal bleeding. The pound's veterinarian performed exploratory surgery. He discovered her spleen had burst and removed it, spaying her at the same time.

When I first saw her, she was lying on the concrete floor of her kennel with a blood-stained white bandage encircling her abdomen. She was a petite long-haired Daschund mix with an elongated body, pointed nose and baleful golden eyes. Tentatively, she looked up at me and reached out with her right front paw. No one had come to claim her, and she was scheduled to be euthanized the following morning – that is, if she made it through the night.

As a representative of S.A.F.E. (Save Animals From Euthanasia), I made regular visits to the pound to rescue adoptable dogs that had been placed on what county kennel workers called the "kill list." Our organization was part of the New Hope program through which non-profit shelters took pets scheduled for euthanasia at the pound, rehabilitated them and placed them in loving homes. Because of her critical injuries, this puppy certainly did not meet our selection criteria.

Still, I knelt down and lifted her gently, cradling her trembling body against my chest. She rested her head on my shoulder and licked me under my chin. I ran my hand along her back, and she whimpered softly. I knew the little dog didn't have much chance of living, but I could not bear the thought of her dying alone and afraid with no one to hold her. For the sake of mercy, I decided to take her home with me.

> "Because of her, I am aware of the small wonders that surround me every day."

S.A.F.E. housed its rescued dogs in kennels at my horse training and breeding facility just north of Phoenix, Arizona. We had room for 38 dogs in pleasant, tree-shaded enclosures with a large, high-walled exercise yard. That first evening, I could not bear to put the little dog in a kennel. I wanted to keep her near me, in case she had trouble during the night. I remembered her reaching helplessly toward me at the pound, and I felt she needed someone to hold her and comfort her now. Showing her I cared might just give her the will to live.

When we got home, I wrapped her in a warm blanket and laid her on my bed. She still whimpered from the pain, so I gave her a baby aspirin along with a dose of a broad-spectrum antibiotic. Replacing the soiled bandage with a clean one, I swabbed the area around her suture with diluted iodine, stroked her gently and allowed her to fall asleep with her head resting on my pillow. When I lay down beside her, she burrowed against my stomach and I could feel the strong beat of her heart. "Ka-chunk! Ka-chunk! Ka-chunk!" Throughout the night, its steady pumping let me know she was alive.

The next morning, she no longer cried, and she seemed more alert. I carried her outside and set her down on the clean, freshly cut grass. In the sun, her wavy black coat glistened like threads of combed silk. "Silky," I said to her, "pretty little Silky."

I took her back inside and gave her another dose of antibiotic. Then I offered her some easily digestible, soft puppy food which she devoured greedily. For the next week, she slept, ate and healed. I fashioned a cozy nest of blankets for her in one corner of my bedroom. Inside it, I placed a stuffed animal and a little rawhide bone. As she grew stronger she began chewing on the bone, holding it delicately between her tiny paws. Her recovery continued, and I removed the bandage from her wound, allowing the air to reach it and speed the healing.

Twice a day, in the morning and in the late afternoon, I took her outside to sit on the sweet-smelling grass. She sniffed the air, and looked up at the vast Arizona sky with wide-eyed wonder. Even though she was weak and suffering, she seemed to enjoy these brief outdoor excursions and came back inside the house with a renewed appetite. Gradually, she began to explore my small front yard.

Two noisy grackles had made a messy, tortilla-shaped nest in the bush outside my bedroom window. Every morning, the birds carried bits of straw, fabric, cotton and string to their building site. Silky discovered this miniature construction project on one of her excursions to the front yard, and she was fascinated by it. She did not try to chase or disturb the birds, but sat and gazed at them for hours. I had never noticed these birds before, even though they slept every night on the other side of the wall, less than three feet from the headboard of my bed.

When she was a bit stronger, I allowed her to follow me to the barn where I always had my morning coffee. As she trotted along beside me, her long hair waved like a hula skirt. Even though she barely had the energy to walk to the barn and back, she flagged her tail and held her head high.

Each day, she wanted to stay outside a while longer. I sat with her underneath a large Palo Verde tree and watched our horse trainer work with the show horses. As she rested by my side with her long ears cocked forward, she listened and observed with great interest.

My veterinarian warned me that the spleen is an organ essential to a dog's immune system. Without it, Silky was vulnerable to all types of life-threatening bacteria and viruses. Her body had minimal ability to fight disease of any kind. "This little dog is practically going to have to live inside a bubble," he said.

So I did my best to create a pleasant, but contained life for her. Silky seemed happy in her tranquil little world. Without the ability to range across a broad territory, she focused on minutiae. Nothing escaped her attention. She explored the ground with her nose and was elated by her discoveries: an old bristle brush that had fallen behind a tack trunk, a bit of cotton, a papery bougainvillea blossom that lay wilting near a stall door, a piece of hoof trimming that had been swept to the back of the grooming area. Like an archaeologist examining bits of pottery uncovered at an ancient dig, she gently pulled the dirt away from each object with her paw, touched it lightly and left it in its place. These were Silky's treasures, special secrets that only she and I shared.

Looking at the world through her eyes, the ordinary became extraordinary. Silky showed such delight in the little things that I had taken for granted or had never noticed at all, things I had rushed by every day. Without realizing it, I became more aware of my immediate surroundings. I heard the soft cooing of doves perched high in the barn's rafters. I watched a pale yellow butterfly dance and dive into the purple-blooming lantana. I picked up a milky chunk of quartz and turned it in my hand, noticing for the first time its thin crimson veins.

Now, more than ever, I believed that Silky was going to survive. By this time, she was housebroken and had learned to sit. She was bright-eyed, inquisitive and full of life. Feathery hairs began to grow on her shaved belly. All that remained of her difficult ordeal was a scar.

During an early morning walk, Silky discovered a beetle crawling along the edge of the concrete barn foundation. She reared on her hind legs, spun around, and gazed up at me with a look of sheer delight.

"Yes," I said to her. "It's alive. It's a little bug."

Silky pushed the beetle with her nose, danced around it and touched it with her paw. When it began to crawl forward, she lay down behind it and watched. As it inched beyond the end of her toenail, she reached out and gently pulled it back. Then, she released it and watched as it began its journey again. She did this several times without harming the fragile creature.

Finally, as if satisfied that she knew all she needed to know about the beetle, she left it and joined me in the tack room as I prepared the morning coffee. I poured myself a cup, then retired to my chair beneath the Palo Verde tree. Silky followed and rested beside me, watching with mild curiosity as the morning barn activities commenced. When I finished my coffee, we walked into the lounge and I deposited the dirty cup in the sink. Then we headed back down the barn aisle toward the house. Halfway along the row of stalls, I heard a whimpering noise and turned to see Silky collapsed in the dirt behind me.

She cried and attempted to scramble to her feet. Quickly, I picked her up and ran toward the house. The little dog gasped for air. Then her whimpering ceased. Her small body went limp in my arms. By the time I reached my front door, Silky's eyes were dull. She had stopped breathing. I attempted to resuscitate her, but I could not.

To this day, I am not certain what happened that morning. Was there an infection harboring inside the little dog? Was there internal bleeding? Or was Silky simply just too frail to live? I will never know the answers to these questions.

We buried her behind the barn, inside the peaceful bubble where she enjoyed her brief life. The next morning, I saw the beetle clawing its determined way along the same narrow strip of concrete. I thought of Silky, and of all the tiny miracles I had never noticed until she came into my life. A pitiful little dog not fit for adoption, she had become one of my greatest teachers. She showed me how to exist in the moment, how to be truly alive. Because of her, I am aware of the small wonders that surround me every day, and I find in them a cause for celebration.

Gail Dudley earned a Master's degree in English Writing at Hollins University. During her 35-year career as a journalist and writer, her stories have appeared in numerous publications and anthologies including *Arizona Highways*, *Phoenix Magazine*, *Artemis*, *The Washington Post* and *Phoenix Home & Garden*. She has always been drawn to animals, especially dogs and horses, and she is the founder of S.A.F.E. (Save Animals from Euthanasia). Her book, *Underdogs: Lessons Learned from Dogs and a Cat Saved at a County Kill Shelter,* is scheduled for publication this winter.

Trouper

Elise Warner

We were filled with enthusiasm and energy, a troupe of stage-struck, starry-eyed and (though not one of us would admit it) slightly home-sick singers and dancers. Our bus and truck company of *Fiorello*, a Broadway and Pulitzer Prize-winning musical, would play 101 cities across the United States and Canada. After months of one, two and three-night stands the cast and crew settled down in Los Angeles for a six-week run. We rented furnished apartments, did our laundry, took dance classes and one day, our leading lady—who loved dogs—asked for a ride to DeWolf's Toyland Kennels in Temple City, California. The kennel, located just outside Los Angeles, bred toy poodles. Five of us just went along for the ride but we all succumbed to puppy love.

My husband, an ex-dancer who became a stage manager, lost his heart to an energetic six-pound, white Toy Poodle with a freckled nose and ears whose fur resembled First Lady Jacqueline Kennedy's bouffant hairstyle. Naturally, we named her Jackie.

One of Jackie's kennel-mates, the elegant Missy, enchanted our lead-ing lady. Sweet and cuddly Debbie beguiled the dance captain and the smallest of the poodles, Big Daddy, made off with her partner. Mimi, a black and white mischief-maker, reeled in a tenor. When the other members of our troupe met our puppies, they too were smitten. Within a week, Mr. Kelly, a Sheltie, and Ming Toy, a Pekinese, had joined the company. By the time we left Los Angeles, a Yorkshire

Jackie

Terrier and two Dachshunds had been added to the entourage. All of the puppies were breeds small enough to adjust easily to hotel rooms and sit comfortably on the buses and trains we used for transportation. Wardrobe trunks now held dog blankets, sweaters, squeaky toys, cans and boxes of dog food and dozens of boots to protect paws from the sidewalk salt when we hit the snows of winter.

"Look! A dog show!" The words greeted us every time the tour bus made a stop. Our star performers were ignored as puppy after puppy left our bus to investigate and rate each rest stop.

When the curtain came down at 11:00 P.M. we'd return to our hotel rooms, unlock the doors and stand back. The race was on. Dogs would chase each other up and down the hotel corridors, in and out of rooms, around and over the furniture and through our legs. During a stop in Washington, D.C., we met a troupe of touring Russian ballerinas. Although the Cold War was far from over, petting and endearments sparked conversation until bodyguards hustled the dancers away. We like to believe the puppies played a small role in the gradual thaw in relations between the two countries.

> "Although the Cold War was far from over, petting and endearments sparked conversation until bodyguards hustled the dancers away."

Jackie, a dancer's companion, became the Pavlova of Poodles; though too shy a dog to tread the boards professionally, she developed the ability to leap from one side of the bus to the other.

Our dogs were the family we needed on the road. They brought the company closer together and made us all less homesick. The cast exchanged feeding and training tips, admired newly clipped and shampooed puppies, celebrated birthdays, and established enduring friendships.

Jackie continued her travels after *Fiorello* closed, accompanying us as we traveled with national tours and industrial shows. She visited Wilmington, Delaware during pre-Broadway try-outs, watched soybeans grow in Waterloo, Iowa when we performed in a show that featured dancing tractors, plows and earth moving equipment and suffered a severe case of indigestion in Hershey, Pennsylvania, when she mistook a bar of chocolate soap for a slab of candy. Between jobs, Jackie practiced *grand jetes*. If we left the dining room to answer the phone, Jackie would spring to the table and devour homemade baked beans or rice pudding—her favorite dishes. On our return, we'd find a happy Poodle, stretched out next to an empty bowl, grinning at us and belching indelicately.

We were rehearsing a musical in Seattle, Washington when Jackie, almost sixteen years old, passed away. She missed our stop at the Kennedy Center in Washington, D.C.; I know she would have enjoyed walks along the Potomac. We were consoled in our grief by cast members, who had loving relationships with their own traveling companions: dogs who understood the adventure to be found on the road; show business gypsies with four paws.

Elise Warner sang, acted and stage managed before becoming addicted to writing. Her articles and short stories have appeared in publications such as *The Washington Post Travel Section, International Living, europeanjournal.de, Literary Traveler, The Gold Prospector* and *The Owl.*

My Sister Samantha, the Pit Bull

Michael DiSchiavi

When I was a freshman in high school, my mother was working as a veterinary assistant, a job she loved. The day after Thanksgiving she got sick with what was, at the time, a mysterious illness. She was in extreme pain on the left side of her head and face; for over a year no one could find the source of the pain. Even after the source was finally discovered to be a benign brain tumor, her pain persisted for almost ten years.

During my freshman year in college, my mother bought a Pit Bull Terrier from a breeder friend. She named the dog Samantha and they bonded instantly. I, on the other hand, was a bit leery at first about having such a dog in the house. However, the breeder assured my mother that Samantha was a pure breed and, since she was getting her as a puppy, Mom could be certain that she had not been trained to fight. Samantha turned out to be extremely friendly and lovable, although very cautious of any strangers coming into the house unless accompanied by someone she already knew.

Samantha quickly trained my mother. She had certain needs and wants and she expected them to be fulfilled at once. Although we teased Mom about this, it turned out that Samantha was the best thing that ever happened to her. Her pain did not go away, but Mom now had a purpose that she did not have before: she had someone who needed her and who demanded that she be there, sick or well.

Samantha became my mother's constant companion. During the many nights when the pain kept her awake, Mom would get up and sit in the living room. Samantha would also get up, staying by Mom until she was ready to go back to bed. If Mom was up all night, Samantha was up all night. If she stayed in bed all day, Samantha stayed in bed all day. For Mom's part, when Samantha wanted to go into the yard, Mom got up to let her out, no matter how sick she felt.

The most powerful example of the bond between them happened when Mom was in the recovery room after one of her many surgeries. Having had general anesthesia too many times, she was having great difficulty waking up. After a while, the recovery room nurses became alarmed. They started shouting at my mother, trying to rouse her, and encouraged me to do the same. Even the other patients present in the room were shouting at her to wake up (presumably so they could go back to sleep). I began saying things to her to trigger a reaction. I told her that my father was hurt, that someone was in the hospital. No response. But when I said, "Samantha is hungry and I don't know where her food is" my mother responded, still in a deep sleep, "It's in the cabinet." We still have not let my mother live that one down.

> "My mother now had a purpose that she did not have before."

When Mom finally became pain free, she and my father began to look forward to finally starting to live again. But that Thanksgiving my father was hospitalized for pneumonia; the admission X-rays found a lung tumor which turned out to be cancer. Thankfully, he survived. But the chemotherapy treatments that saved his life left him weak and very depressed. Once again, it was Samantha who came to the rescue.

Once Dad he came home from the hospital, he sat in his favorite arm-chair for most of the day, every day. Samantha saw how lethargic he was becoming and she took action. Every time Dad would get off the chair, no matter how briefly, Samantha would run to the chair and sit in it. When he would return, she would have her eyes closed and pretend to be sleeping. The pattern was set: he would try to get her up, she would growl at him and he'd let her stay on the chair. It was her way of getting him up and around, and making him laugh. This behavior was not her normal routine, but it lasted for the entire time my father was sick. As soon as he got better, she stopped stealing his seat. The doctors saved my father's life, but Samantha kept him going.

Eventually, Samantha became older and slower. One day my father found her dead in her favorite corner of her bedroom (my former bedroom had long since become Samantha's room). My parents were devastated; Mom cradled Samantha in her arms for hours. Samantha's spirit is still with them, though. Two years later, Mom adopted a macaw parrot she named Lola whom she loves dearly. However, as much as my mother treasures (and spoils) Lola, she still looks lovingly at the professional portrait she had made of Samantha when she was in her prime. Every day she gets sad when she looks at that portrait but she would never, ever think of taking it down.

Michael DiSchiavi teaches English at John Dewey High School in Brooklyn, New York. He has authored essays and book reviews appearing in various journals.

Angel in Disguise

Crystal Calderon

When I was 12, I was molested by my stepfather. I had been violated. I was devastated, confused, and vulnerable. I was supposed to be entering eighth grade in the fall, in my hometown. Instead, I was sent to live with my grandparents far away from the "danger."

It was while I was living there that Sandy came to me: a dog that simply showed up day after day, spent time with me, and then departed. A Golden Retriever, she had beautiful auburn hair that reminded me of fall leaves. When I looked into her bright, clear eyes, I saw compassion and kindness. Sandy had a magnetism that drew me to her from the start, and our personalities simply clicked. It seemed to me that Sandy had a clear understanding of what I was going through during that very difficult time. She helped me to forget the very real pain that I had trouble sharing with anyone else, and her friendship brought me the peace and solace I couldn't find on my own.

I never questioned why Sandy decided to befriend me. She came to see me daily, yet I never gave it a second thought. Instead, I accepted her friendship, found comfort in it and allowed her to help me lick my wounds. We would often go for walks in the woods. Sometimes we would sit on the porch together and find comfort in the silence. Sandy helped me find my strength to get through this horrible injustice, the changes, the unfamiliar place. She was neither judgmental nor interested in the awful details. She simply made me feel safe and loved.

Unconditionally. When I met her I was alone in the world. Her presence instantly filled that void.

She was my angel in disguise, my gift sent from God. I know, now, that God brought Sandy into my life to help me heal. He knew that His little girl had been emotionally scarred and needed someone to help her mend. God knew that my wounds were deep, that my young heart was broken, my spirit crushed. He knew that my faith in mankind, at that time in my life, had been shattered. Man, in human form, had failed me, had abused my innocence.

> "Sandy helped me find my strength to get through this horrible injustice."

So God sent me "man's best friend."

Sandy is gone now. I am confident that in Heaven she has found a special place. How could she not have? Her commitment to me during my time of need was true, unwavering. I will be forever grateful for her loyal companionship. Where she came from is still a mystery.

Or perhaps not.

_____

Crystal Calderon lives in Smyrna, Delaware with her husband, Louis. She is the mother of five children, and grandmother of four, all boys.

The New Me

Kathleen Gerard

I've heard it said that when you make a conscious decision to get a dog, you don't get the dog you want, but rather, you get the dog you need. Such was the case of Sissy's entrance into my life.

Throughout most of my twenties I lay wrapped in the cocoon of a ten-by-twelve foot bedroom in my mother's house. There had been thirteen surgeries and seventeen years of disability (and counting) to combat degenerating bones and soft tissue ruptures in my feet and ankles, and a slew of subsequent complications, including cancer. Some days it felt as though I were stuck in a cage, a prison. I kicked and screamed and railed against my fate.

Over the course of my disability, friends had gotten on with their lives: advanced degrees, career booms, marriages, divorces, families, houses and children. I felt alone, stuck, as though I were in a state of inertia. Yes, all the time off my feet had helped my writing career to flourish. But then a dear friend of mine said in passing, "When is all this surgery nonsense going to be over? When am I finally going to get the old Kathy back?" Something in the words rattled me to the core. The healthy life I had once taken for granted—and the one I had envisioned for myself—had vanished. The old Kathy was gone, and the sad fact was, she wasn't coming back.

But who was the new Kathy?

Sissy

I was now halfway through my thirties. I felt broken and damaged inside and out. Riddled with insecurity because of the limitations imposed by my disability, I had shrunk away from people because I felt I could no longer meet their expectations. "You're too isolated," my mother said one day. "What can you do to help yourself? What would bring you joy?"

Joy? The word instantly conjured my love for dogs, especially my fondness for Yorkshire Terriers. I had grown up with one, and another had kept me very good company in the early days of my disability. However, when Yorkie Number Two passed away, I felt I wasn't physically able to care for a new puppy. But by now, I was semi-mobile again. Maybe it was time. Maybe the unconditional love of a canine companion was exactly what I needed.

I started perusing classified ads and the internet. I contacted breeders and rescue centers. My homebound self suddenly felt inspired and motivated whenever I fastened my leg braces, reached for my crutches and dropped in at pet shops. I checked out at least a dozen dogs over the next six months, but I couldn't find a match. There were cost issues, dogs that had been sold before I got to them, health issues that made puppies unsellable, dogs too big or excitable for me to manage, or I simply "didn't fall in love," as they say. I began to wonder if a new dog was really the answer. Although I had voiced those feelings, deep down I didn't believe them. Maybe the journey—the search in and of itself—was the real benefit. It had gotten me out of the house and back into the world on some level. Maybe the timing just wasn't right.

Eight months later and a hundred and thirty-seven miles from home, I finally found Sissy. Through a friend of a friend I discovered a breeder/broker who imported Yorkshire Terriers from Brazil. When I contacted the breeder, she suggested I come for a visit and scope out her latest charges. I tried not to be too hopeful, as it seemed a long shot, but my mother—a tireless, patient good sport—took on the two-hour drive.

When we walked into the breeder's house, we were greeted by close to thirty Yorkies waiting to find homes. Yet none stole my heart enough to make a ten to fifteen-year commitment. Just as I was about to give up, my mother suggested we scour the list of available pups one last time. When we cross-catalogued names and identification numbers, we realized there was one puppy we hadn't seen. When I inquired about her, the breeder hesitated. "Oh, I don't think you'd really want *her*. She has some issues, she's very shy…."

I looked at my mother, and she looked at me. We both knew I was an expert on shyness, among other neuroses. I shrugged and said, "What have we got to lose?"

The breeder scoured the pack. She went to the farthest corner of the dog pen, and, peeling sleeping puppies off one another and checking their tags, she finally uncovered a little runt. She was squashed and disheveled-looking, quivering and hiding at the bottom of the stack. She batted her eyes to the light a few times and looked around as if completely lost, but, in fact, she'd been found. We both had!

Sissy and I have been together three years. I'm convinced my Yorkshire Terrier must have lived a past life as a cat. For starters, Sissy loves fish: tuna, cod, and salmon are among her favorites. And she'll play for hours, chasing a tiny mouse on a string, if I'm willing to keep moving the bait. But the most notable feline quality about my dog is her tendency to hide. Long before I even reach for her leash or put on my coat, she must read my mind and sense that our departure is imminent. She tucks her tail and skulks away like a CIA operative. At five pounds, it's easy for Sissy to vanish. And it's even easier for her to elude me, as whenever I spot her in full covert operation mode and try to sneak up and grab her, she quickly darts away, just out of reach.

> "I'm convinced my Yorkshire Terrier must have lived a past life as a cat."

I've tried just about everything to break her of this habit. Furniture has been moved, blockaded. Treats dangled. And I hate to admit it, but I've even resorted to exiting the house and ringing the outside doorbell in the hope that the idea of a potential visitor will coax her out of seclusion. All these lures might work once or twice, but Sissy catches on quickly.

It's become sort of an exasperating game, a challenge, a battle of wills. But maybe it goes deeper than that. Maybe there's truth in the adage *you don't get the dog you want, you get the dog you need.* I've come to believe that I need Sissy as much as she needs me. We are two of kind. We're both creatures who often hide from the world and people in it, but we've forged a bond. A necessary bond. Every time I'm successful in outsmarting and capturing her, and I slip on her leash and we step out together, I feel as though I can breathe again, as if I've been resurrected and liberated from all those years I spent in the tiny cocoon of my room. I don't know if it's her size or spunk or just the wag of her tail, but people and other dogs seem to naturally gravitate toward her. Once I can wrangle her from seclusion, Sissy is warm and friendly and trusting—and that's contagious. That five-pound little ball of fur has drawn me out of my shell and taught me how to finally live again, with joy and acceptance, as the new me.

Kathleen Gerard's fiction was awarded the Perillo Prize for Italian-American Writing and was nominated for Best New American Voices, a national prize in literature. Her work has appeared in *Calyx, The Crescent Review, Italian Americana, Art Times, Storyteller Magazine,* and elsewhere. She is a contributing columnist to Northern New Jersey's largest newspaper, *The Record, Our Sunday Visitor* and *Catholic Twin Circle* magazines.

Guide Dogs
Margaret Whitford

Writer Edward Hoagland once suggested that the key to enjoying a dog is not found in making the dog semi-human, but in trying to become partly dog. But what would it mean to emulate my Jack Russell Terriers? Would I have to embrace digging as a vocation?

Each spring, Gilbert and Annie collaborated on the digging of a tunnel in the side of a small hill in the backyard. I called it the "summer residence," because they'd disappear into its cool darkness during the hottest part of the day. Gilbert was the project's foreman, while Annie did most of the work. He'd nudge her aside periodically to inspect progress, barking continuously (commands, I assume), and then let her continue. Occasionally, she'd lie on her side to use all four feet to dig. Despite the complications of having to wash her earth-encrusted head, I always considered this maneuver a sign of superior intelligence.

My husband Tom and I have been their guardians since bringing each home at nine weeks of age, Annie arriving ten months after Gilbert. Had we known more about these "little thugs in clown suits," as the *Wall Street Journal* once characterized them, we might not have chosen Jack Russell Terriers, for they are, to put it mildly, a handful. But they quickly burrowed into our hearts, and we were helpless to resist.

In a way, Gilbert broke us in for Annie, challenging our equilibrium from the very first. Within hours of joining our family, he launched himself off a four foot-high stone wall and landed on his head in the

Gilbert and Annie

middle of our asphalt driveway. In light of his subsequent contortions, I feared he'd broken his neck. But then he righted himself, gave a vigorous shake, and continued down the driveway toward some goal he seemed determined to reach. Jack Russell Terriers are known for this kind of single-mindedness.

It's the same drive he'd apply to games, retrieving a thrown lacrosse ball for ages. I once warned a friend not to start tossing the ball unless he was willing to play indefinitely. In the absence of an obvious game, Gilbert would transform chores into sport. In winter, he loved catching the snow as it left the shovel. He'd hurl himself at the back door until I let him out to join Tom. It took some skill to avoid clipping him under the chin, or hitting him on the head, since he tried to bite the snow before it was airborne. Raking leaves invariably commanded his attention, as he leapt into the growing mounds, scattering leaves everywhere.

I think his love of play was an outgrowth of his confidence. He was the only male in his litter, and seemed born with a sense of his preeminence. He took up more space than his sisters, even though they were larger. In contrast, Annie was the only female in a litter of large males. She had to struggle for her place, and so arrived with something to prove. Games never interested her much, unless they represented a chance at domination.

In any other family, Annie might very well have been the Alpha dog, because of her intelligence and assertiveness. But because Gilbert arrived first and possessed such self-assurance, Annie rarely challenged him. I feared that would change as Gilbert became frail with age, but it didn't. In fact, Annie grew protective, chirping to him in the backyard until she saw him on the path to come inside, allowing him to trample on her as he settled in for the night. Compassionate is the only word I have for her behavior, and in this, I think she surpasses me.

Gilbert died two years ago, three months into his sixteenth year, in early fall, on a day that held the last of summer's warmth. I believe he chose his time, resisting our efforts to comfort him until I wrapped him in towels and brought him to the vet. Despite all that time took from him, he retained a wellspring of sweetness, as if he had faith in life's goodness, in my love. I wonder if I will be able to grow old with as much grace and large-heartedness.

"He's comfortable now, let me give you some time alone with him," our vet said. Tom and I held hands as we petted him, each trying to preserve in memory the texture of his broken coat, the pressure of his heart beating against our hands. I was so close to telling the vet we'd changed our minds, but ultimately, we asked her to return and administer the drug that would stop his heart. At the end, his body was so light, like a winged seed or feather.

That night I dreamed of him. I felt him walk up my side of the bed, nudge the covers up, and nestle into me, the way he used to when he was younger, his back fitting snugly against the curve of my stomach. It was as though he wanted to offer comfort, wanted me to understand I needed to release him.

> "Gilbert taught me about letting go, even as Annie shows me how to hold on."

Annie remains beautiful, even as she nears seventeen. Her finely boned head is black except for a white stripe running down her forehead. A splash of darkness adorns one shoulder and a black heart covers the back of one foot. It's like a valentine she offers as she departs. She is graying in such a way that white rings encircle her eyes, making her appear like she's wearing a mask. Oddly enough, it tends to make her look earnest, as glasses can affect a youthful face. I love the way she smells, especially the pads of her feet. They have a warm scent like baked bread, laced with nutmeg.

I cannot look at her without remembering her youth. When I hear her labored climb up our stairs, I think of her leaping up to attack the hose whenever I watered the garden. She wanted to wrest the nozzle from my hand, and as I held it higher, she'd bound ever upwards. I only stopped the contest when she started resembling an inflated blowfish. When she ran, she looked like Superman's sidekick, front and back paws fully extended. She needed only a cape to complete the image. There was such vitality to her movement; it never failed to make me happy.

Annie's good days still outnumber her bad, and I don't believe she is in pain. Mild arthritis in her spine leaves her stiff sometimes, but the medicine we give her helps. There are things she no longer does. She can't descend the wooden stairs or climb onto our bed at night. I wish I could have noted the last time she did any of these things, for I won't see them again.

As she hovers near the couch where I sit, there is a mixture of longing and reluctance in her eyes. She wants to join me, but is afraid of pain when I lift her. "Come on Annie, come on little girl," I coo, extending my arms to her. Eventually, she will venture within reach, and I will raise her into softness, her warm familiar weight a comfort as I read.

When she was younger, walking her was like exercising a moth. She'd flit from one thing to another, always in a hurry, always straining at her lead. Now, I frequently must rouse her from sleep for these outings, but she always wants to come with me. She pours herself off the couch, stumbling until she regains her footing. It's hard to describe how moving I find her efforts, her refusal to forego the possibility of joy.

Once we're outside, she still strives to be first, until fatigue forces her to moderate her pace and walk beside me. Sometimes, I'll quicken my step to urge a response, and she'll start to run in her rocking-horse way. There is delight in her gait, an eagerness for discovery. It's a leaning into life I'd like to emulate, especially as I grow older. Old age has the capacity to scare me. I am too aware of what is no longer possible, of the choices that are no longer mine to make. There is less time ahead than behind me, and, sometimes, I am disheartened by that scarcity.

I am a witness to the arcs of my dogs' lives. I've watched their boundless energy succumb to the constraints of old age, and, finally, death. At each stage, Gilbert and Annie simply carried on, without regret for what was lost to them. Their approach suggests something about how to live.

Gilbert taught me about letting go, even as Annie shows me how to hold on. And that may be what life is about, especially as we age, a flowing and balancing between what is no longer ours to keep and what still remains.

Margaret Whitford holds a Bachelor of Arts degree from the University of Pennsylvania, a Masters in Business Administration from The Wharton School, and a Masters in Fine Arts from Chatham University. Chatham

University nominated her work for the Association of Writing Program's *Intro Journals Project*, December 2007, and awarded her the *Best Thesis* in Creative Nonfiction for her thesis *Traveling Home*. She divides her time between homes in Pittsburgh and Provence that she shares with her husband and dog. She is at work on a collection of essays exploring the challenges of adapting to life in rural France.

The Shifting Carpet

Heather Allison

"Taylor's not feeling well today," Lian, his mother, told me when I went to collect the boy for the afternoon. My heart sank. We'd had some very happy days during the last six weeks, since Taylor's first round of treatment had finished, playing with the train set and making up stories together. No one could tell us how the next round of therapy would affect him, but they had warned us it was going to be rough, so we were all making the most of this precious time. I felt a wave of dread surge though my body and I swallowed down the bile that had risen to my mouth.

"Oh... I'm sorry to hear that," I replied, with a light but sympathetic tone, or at least I hope that's how it sounded. "If you like, I could play with you here today instead. I could read you stories."

"No, he wants to go to your house. He's looking forward to seeing the dogs, aren't you, Tay?" Taylor responded with a nod. I swallowed and searched my fuddled brain for something suitable to say. It was lovely that Taylor trusted me enough to take him away from his Mum, but the responsibility weighed heavily on my shoulders. This was the first time he'd looked as ill as this.

"He hasn't eaten a single thing and he's had nothing to drink," Lian explained. I looked at him and smiled encouragement, entering into the game of let's pretend, that it was completely normal for a four year-old to choose to be "nil by mouth." I shuddered as this phrase ran

Maizie and Honey

through my head. He'd been "nil by mouth" on his fourth birthday in February, while all the rest of children in the ward had party food in his honor. Those were very dark days. *Don't think about that,* I told myself, not now. *Concentrate on the present.*

Looking at Taylor, I couldn't help but think that he'd surely prefer to be tucked up in bed, or snuggling down on the sofa in the sleeping bag I bought for him. He looked so wick. He'd lost so much weigh. His pale face seemed dominated by those big, beautiful eyes, circled today with smudgy grey rings. I silently prayed, "Please help me. Give me the strength to stay strong, to remain outwardly cheerful and optimistic and above all else, don't let me break down and cry in front of him."

I helped Tay to the car and lifted him into the booster seat I keep ready for him in the back. I could hear my voice sounding falsely cheerful, but how could it not be false. For years, part of my job had been encouraging surgery patients, but now, as I tried to tempt a positive response from Taylor, those days seemed a lifetime ago. Nothing I suggested—burgers, chicken nuggets, toys—roused any response from Taylor other than a resigned "No," and it was clearly an effort for him to utter that one small word.

We pulled into the drive and I turned off the engine.

"You wait here Tay; I'll take the shopping in and let Honey out to see you, like I did last week. I'll leave Maizie in her crate until you're settled, we don't want her barging into you, do we?"

I couldn't think of any other way of doing it: if I'd taken Tay in first, the dogs might have knocked him off balance. It wouldn't have taken much to send him flying. I unlocked the front door and was greeted by Honey, my eight year-old Golden Retriever. She has always been a "talker" and her greeting today was especially welcoming.

> "The dogs never deserted their posts by his side: a head rested on each of his little bruised legs, and four hopeful eyes watched his every move."

"Taylor's come to play. Go and see him." Honey trotted out to the car, tail wagging, and I could hear her greeting him. She leaves no doubt in anyone's mind that she's pleased to see them. I rushed through to the kitchen with the bags. I was less than a minute, but as I got back to the front door, I could see to my dismay that Taylor had released himself and was trying to get to Honey. I had to hold both his hands to stop him from toppling over, but he pulled one free to stroke Honey's head as she walked protectively by his side into the house.

"She likes that," I told him.

"Does she?" he asked, and relief flowed through me as he looked up and smiled.

"She's very pleased to see you."

I remember a saying on a poster at work: "You can learn to dance on a shifting carpet." I have thought about those words many times since January, when the reason for Tay's headaches and his wobbly walk was first discovered and we embarked on this harrowing journey. When he first lost his hair, I didn't think that I'd ever grow used to how he looked. His beautiful, curling auburn hair has been gone for a while now. His little head looks so vulnerable without it.

But Taylor is an amazing little boy. I'm not related to him at all, at least not by blood. When his family and I try to explain our relationship to people who don't know us, we see their faces glaze over in confusion, as our connection is so complicated. No matter, I'm Taylor's Grandma and I love him and he loves me, although I'm beginning to think that the attraction in coming to our house is not so much the train set, the baking or the sticking and painting. More and more I believe that it is our two dogs.

Within minutes of Taylor coming through the door today, he was not only smiling but laughing at the dogs as they carefully circled him, gently beating him with their wagging tails. I watched with delight as Maizie, our eleven month-old black Labrador, treated him with the utmost respect and affection, instinctively knowing that her usual exuberant greeting would be inappropriate.

"Stop barking, Maizie," he said. Looking at Taylor now, I could see his color changing from an unhealthy-looking murky grey to a pale peachy pink. His expression was animated now too, where minutes before it had been blank. He bent towards Maizie as he spoke and she gave his cheek a quick lick. He started to giggle. That little sound, that at one time we'd all taken for granted, was the most wonderful sound I had ever heard.

"Grandma's starving," I told him, not wanting to break the spell, but not wanting to draw too much attention to his change of mood, either. "Will you be alright while I make myself a sandwich?"

"I'll be fine, I'll just play with the doggies," he said in his precise, measured voice.

I was glad to escape to the kitchen, feeling my emotions beginning to get the better of me. I listened with pleasure to Taylor chatting to the dogs while I made the lunch with his favorite bread, cutting his sandwich up small to make it look less intimidating, remembering domestic science lessons about how to tempt an invalid to eat.

"I've made you some lunch if want it Tay. It doesn't matter if you don't." This was a lie of course. He desperately needed to eat; how else was he to gain the strength he needed to fight this evil disease.

"I am quite hungry, actually," he said, settling himself at the table, with a dog on either side of him. He chuckled, amused by the looks on their eager faces as they anticipated that some of the food might be heading their way. We both used antiseptic hand gel, and I was pleased to see how seriously he took this task, working the liquid expertly between his fingers and the backs of his hands, just as I'd shown him. As much as I love my dogs I'm always aware of infection control, and Taylor is especially vulnerable.

I could feel myself starting to relax. Watching Taylor eat his sandwich with enjoyment and then letting me make him another one, which disappeared the same way, gave me immense pleasure. The dogs never deserted their posts by his side: a head rested on each of his little bruised legs, and four hopeful eyes watched his every move. This amused him greatly, and from time to time he'd flick them the smallest of crumbs. He delighted in watching as they searched the carpet for the offering.

Taylor laughed and talked, his color now fully restored and his eyes alight with pleasure. We went on to have a lovely afternoon together, the four of us. What I saw my dogs achieve, just by being dogs, was a miracle, a little one on the scale of all that has been done for Taylor, but a miracle nonetheless.

Heather Allison lives in Southport on the western coast of England. She and her husband have three children, three step-children and four precious grand-children. She has been writing for four years and has had two short stories read on BBC Radio.

Angel Therapy

Sherri A. Stanczak

My youngest son just told me that he is moving out in a few months. This is his first year of college and he wants to experience his independence. Even though I'm very proud of him for working, for saving money and for wanting to be on his own, it still makes me feel sad. All three of my boys will be on their own now. My boys have always kept me going. I don't know how to live my life without them.

And not only am I going through the empty-nest syndrome, but I am also faced with a lot of my own health issues, including multiple sclerosis and permanent damage to my sciatic nerve from spinal surgery. I've lived with chronic pain for some time, and am on so much medication now, including morphine, that I'm not able to work or drive anymore. If ever there was someone who needed visits from an angel, it's me.

And that's just what happened. A very kind man who works with my father and breeds Yorkshire Terriers decided I needed a puppy. My husband, Mike, wasn't so sure. He remembered being crushed when his own dogs died, and he wanted to spare me that. And we have an active lifestyle despite my ailments, he was afraid a puppy would limit us. But when I saw this special puppy, I just had to have her. I fell in love with Angel the moment I laid eyes on her.

Angel makes me laugh. She makes my heart melt when she looks at me and cuddles up next to my body. About a month ago, I had a bad time when I had to inject a steroid medication each day through an

Angel

intravenous needle. Angel knew something was wrong with me. With a concerned look, she stared at the I. V. and then checked out my arm, back and forth, for a long time. Then she came up on the couch with me and licked my arm. She never left my side the whole time. She was such a comfort to me. Another time, the pain was so severe that I began crying. Angel jumped up on my lap, trying to figure out what to do for me. She actually started licking my tears. I couldn't help but smile. What a special puppy I have! She has blessed my life so much in so many ways.

Angel won me over at first wag, but she had to work on Mike. Not for long. She meets him at the door with the warmest greeting every day.

She also wakes him up each morning with so much excitement. As her tiny tail wags, she dances in a circle on her hind legs and pats his leg with her front paws. He can't resist bending over to pet her, and then she jumps into his arms and licks his face and hands. No one has ever been that excited to see him. She hasn't slowed us down either. She has become quite a boating dog.

Angel has definitely livened up our household. They say that laughter is the best medicine, and thanks to this amazing puppy I can tell you it is literally true. She has given me a reason to get out of bed each morning, even on those days when the pain is so great that it's hard to get up. Since I have gotten her, I have even been able to quit taking a couple of my medications. I know it's because of Angel. She has a tendency to keep me a little more active, and she has put a permanent smile on my face.

> "Angel won me over at first wag, but she had to work on Mike."

She has taken my mind off my pain and she has given me a reason to keep on trying. She has been great therapy for me.

I really do believe in angels. I believe God puts them here on earth to help us through our trials or guide us in the right direction. My Angel has definitely done that for me. She has been a true inspiration in my life. I am thankful to the breeders who gave me the dog and my mom and dad for making this happen for me. I am also thankful for my husband, Mike, for giving in to my special need. Of course, Angel has her own way of thanking him every day.

Sherri Stanczak lives in Missouri and is the mother of three boys. She has published a book, *From the Heart of a Mother*, and her writing has appeared in publications including *Missouri Life*, *Heartland Boating Magazine* and *River Hills Traveler*.

Miracles at the Other End of the Leash

Nancy A. Hoke

It was an unusual scene: a boy on his belly, spread out on a mat in the school gym, reading to a little white dog. The two seemed oblivious to the rest of the activity in the gym as they lay side by side, noses in the picture book. Being the handler who held Maggie's leash, I sat quietly to the side. Around the gym were other dogs and their handlers, teachers and classroom aides, and children in various locations reading to the dogs who regularly visit this emotional support classroom. Regularly scheduled reading assistance from registered therapy dogs was making a significant difference for these children in their reading progress as well as in their behavior.

Maggie, a West Highland White Terrier, was the cutest puppy we had ever brought into our home. She came to live with my husband, Gene, and me two months after my retirement, and easily became the focus of our attention. Our children had always been the primary playmates for legions of family pets over the years, but this time the puppy had only the two of us. In an effort to be responsible, we enrolled our puppy in training classes for the first time. It was fun to learn about the how and why of normal canine behavior, and during "Puppy Kindergarten," we learned that Westies are all about play. Plans for a second Westie began to make sense to us.

Maggie and Max

Seven week-old Max was exactly six months younger than Maggie, and we soon had them on the same training schedule, enrolled in the same obedience classes. During this time, we explored volunteer opportunities with pets, and learned dogs make great "therapists" for people in a variety of settings. The search for more information began, and we found there are therapy dog organizations that test, observe, and register dogs for this kind of work. Gene was not yet retired, but the idea of doing volunteer work with the two dogs we had come to love was very appealing to us. Within a few months, we had two well-trained "lap dogs" with lots of energy, and we learned about Kindly Canines, a local dog therapy group.

My entire professional career had been committed to working with children, first as a hospital-based pediatric nurse, then as a certified school nurse in public elementary schools. Gene had always enjoyed our own children as well as the time we spent as youth leaders in our church and community. When we learned of research that documented how children can improve reading skills by regularly reading to dogs, our path was chosen.

The concept was unknown to school officials at first, but we entered into a pilot program in one of the elementary schools. We obtained all required testing and clearances, and within two years' time we had several teams of handlers and dogs begin their visits to classrooms. Max and Maggie knew that putting on their special vest meant they were "going to work," and we saw them become as excited and committed to this work as we were.

Since then, the changes we see in children who have visits from therapy dog teams are both impressive and humbling. Yes, reading scores have increased more than expected when documented by pre and post-testing. However, it is the children who respond so positively and show us the value of this work. We, the handlers, sit with leash in hand, as kids lose themselves in reading. They are not self-conscious, and have total acceptance from their reading buddies. Mistakes go unnoticed, and confidence grows with skill in this non-judgmental relationship between child and dog.

Once we were in a classroom for the last visit of the school year. Max was with Gene, and a new student, Jerry, went over with a thick book, sat on the floor, and began reading aloud as he petted Max. When it was time to read to another dog, Jerry continued to read to Max. Other children rotated among the dogs and handlers during the remainder of class time, but the teachers allowed Jerry to stay with Max the entire hour, and the reading continued.

A few weeks later, I spoke with a remedial teacher from his previous school and learned Jerry had severe emotional trauma that resulted in his placement in the classroom we visited.

"Jerry never wanted to be touched, and refused to read aloud. He didn't actually read aloud, did he?" When she heard Jerry had indeed read aloud to Max, tears began streaming down her face. The power of this simple relationship would become the key to healing for Jerry.

> "Mistakes go unnoticed, and confidence grows with skill in this non-judgmental relationship between child and dog."

Ronna had severe self-esteem issues that interfered with her confidence in all social settings. Max and Maggie were the two dogs she loved to read to when we visited her classroom. She sat on the floor to read as she petted them, oblivious to the other activity in the classroom. Two thirds of the way through the school year, she came to a session with our teams and brought a story about puppies she had not only written herself, but had also illustrated. Ronna enthusiastically read to Maggie, and pointed out details in the illustrations. Puppies had casts and bandages, smiles and tears, and they made faces to express their emotion.

We saw a transformation in this child during the year, and knew we now had the perfect opportunity to show Ronna how very special she was. I conceived the idea to get this book bound, and for her to donate a copy to the local animal shelter. The teacher was eager to help, and offered to get the book ready as I enlisted outside support for the project. We dedicated the end of the school year to make it all happen.

During that time, I attended a writer's conference and showed Ronna's book to several published author friends who wrote notes of praise to her, notes that also encouraged her to continue writing. When Ronna realized the special meaning of those notes, her teacher allowed her the opportunity to see books by those authors in the library, and Ronna began to demonstrate a new strength in personality, confidence, and performance. The day she stood with Max and Maggie and made her presentation to the animal shelter in the presence of her family and friends, we saw a young girl standing tall and proud. A photograph published in the local paper explained the event, but the meaning proved to be much greater than that presentation. The following year Ronna managed to excel in both academic and social areas to the point that she was moved out of the special education classroom, no longer needed personal assistance, and became the author of published poetry. Her teachers and personal assistant have no doubt that this change began when Ronna gained confidence and acceptance by reading to the dogs who visited her classroom.

Over time, it has been a surprise to see our own and other family pets demonstrate such a profound sense of purpose. They consistently meet unspoken needs for help, comfort, and unconditional love without expectation of reward. We have seen Max and Maggie sense and respond to human need that has escaped even professional observers, something as simple as a need to be touched. The response to their interaction becomes the first clue to us, the human bystanders.

Gene and I started work with therapy dogs believing *we* were the volunteers who would be doing the work. In our minds, it was a side benefit that we could take our dogs with us. What we learned is that ours is the privilege to prepare and make possible the visits, then step back and watch. The work, love, and miracles happen at the other end of the leash.

Nancy Hoke is the wife of Gene, mother of three married daughters, grandmother of nine, and "Mom" to three registered and one soon-to-be registered therapy dogs. She is a retired registered nurse, former counselor and psychotherapist, and now pursues writing along with volunteer work in her church and community.

Susie

Maggie Flynn

When I was 17, my mother read my journal—one of the biggest viola-
tions of trust a teenage girl can endure. I would not have found out
about this had my mother not read in its pages a violation of her own
faith in me, in the form of an entry about my having tried marijuana
for the first time. After a couple days of suffering my mother's silent
treatment, I asked her what was wrong. She told me what she had
done, and my anger quickly escalated to match hers. We reached an
impasse. Both of us were suffering from a breach of the other's trust,
and neither would apologize. This likely would have gone on for days,
if it hadn't been for Susie, the family dog.

We rescued Susie from the shelter when I was eight years old, after seeing her picture in the paper. A black and white Fox Terrier mix with
brown cheeks, a long curly tail, and a proclivity for covering every surface
with which she came into contact with black hairs, Susie quickly became
my best friend. We got Susie after moving into a new house in Marshall,
Michigan, where I would be starting at a new school in the fall. An only
child, I was somewhat shy and introspective around my classmates and
didn't make friends easily. I took great comfort in coming home from a
day filled with anxiety over whether I would find a game to join at recess
to seeing Susie jumping three feet into the air to welcome me home.

Susie was the sort of extremely patient dog who would let me dress her
up in my doll clothes without so much as a yip. My whole family

Susie

adored her. She was the impetus for our nightly walks and a constant source of comic relief whether she was racing in circles around the yard or shaking with desire every time she spotted a squirrel through the front picture window. As the years progressed, she became not only a beloved pet, but also a means of keeping peace within the family.

The afternoon my mother came clean about reading my journal, I'd barricaded myself in my bedroom. A few hours into the standoff, my father knocked on the door. "Let's take Susie for a walk," he said. I dried my eyes, opened my bedroom door, and nodded. I was grateful to the dog for giving us an excuse to momentarily escape the dense emotions in our home. Surely my dad was, too. Whenever my mom and I had a blowup, he walked a fine line, pleading each offended party's case to the other.

On that particular walk, my father's advice was pretty straightforward: "Maybe you shouldn't be writing about things that you don't want your mother to know." I conceded this was true, but felt as if my dad was missing the point. I'd considered my journal a place for private, uncensored reflection, and if my mother hadn't violated that sacred space, then we wouldn't have been in such a tense situation.

Susie pulled on her leash, likely picking up on a squirrel's scent, and dragged me over to the side of the road. She wasn't a model of good behavior when we took her for walks, barking and standing on her hind legs when she saw other dogs, dragging when she got tired, and refusing to walk in a straight line. In fact, my family had never spent a lot of effort disciplining Susie in general. If company refused to pet her, she'd bark at them through their whole visit. She begged for food at every meal by standing on her hind legs and propping herself on the corner of our chairs, moving from me, her easiest target, to my dad, and finally to my mom, the slowest eater of the group. What she lacked in manners, though, she made up for in her sweet disposition. She was a good dog, and my parents' idea of discipline had never been preemptive.

Similarly, my mom thought of me as a good kid, and she always enjoyed indulging me. She'd allow me to watch all the television I wanted during my summer vacations, let me rule the car tape deck when the family went out to dinner or on a day trip. My mother had never even given me a curfew; I simply had to call and let her know where I was and when I'd be home. I, in turn, had started stretching my boundaries, as teens do, thrilled at the notions of freedom and experimentation.

"I've read your journal from time to time," my mother told me earlier that day, "and up until now I've never seen anything that concerned me."

At the time I assumed she was cruelly reading in hopes of catching me in some deviant act, but in retrospect I'm sure that wasn't her intent.

My mother was overstepping that boundary hoping for reassurance. She read because she assumed her notions would be reinforced: I was a good kid with good friends who had been well warned of the dangers of drinking, drugs, and sex, and I would certainly have the wherewithal to resist any temptations coming my way. My mother always held me in such high esteem that she was baffled when I no longer fit her picture, and she couldn't have reacted with anything but hurt and anger.

My dad and I extended our walk, neither of us in any rush to get back to the house. I watched Susie stop to sniff an intriguing patch of grass, so unaffected by the family drama. As always, Susie's presence made me feel as if things weren't so bad. My mother wasn't an evil, unsympathetic spy; she had her side and I had mine, and maybe we were both a little right and a little wrong. When we got back from the walk, my mom was fixing dinner. I stood behind her at the oven and told her I was sorry, and we began the process of letting go of the whole incident.

This of course wasn't the only time my mother and I faced off during my teen years, and every time we fought, it was Susie who gave me perspective on the incident. The very fact that she wagged her tail ferociously at both of us was always a reminder that my mother hadn't suddenly morphed into a controlling, unreasonable being. She was the same mom my dog and I loved dearly, and it must have been me bringing out those aspects of her personality. On those days when it seemed that no understanding could be reached, and I felt as if my parents were ready to wash their hands of me, I always had the respite of escaping out the door with Susie. Grabbing her leash from the stairwell and seeing her excitement gave me the certainty that someone still loved and wanted to be around me, even when I was at my worst.

Once I went away to college, some of the tensions that had developed my last couple years of living at home started to recede. I had more of the freedom I so craved, and could appreciate spending a weekend at home each month as a break from the noise and lack of space in the dorm. When I brought friends home with me, they were always surprised by the picture on the refrigerator of a grade school-aged me holding Susie up on her hind legs, showing her off in a pink doll dress.

"That's the same dog?" they'd ask. "She doesn't look that old."

They were right. She was still spry, working up a jump or two when we came to the door, but I noticed the changes, the white spots on her face that used to be brown, the cataracts making her eyes look like shiny marbles. The summer after I graduated from college and was getting ready to move to Nashville, Tennessee, to join an AmeriCorps program, I received a call from my mom. Susie had been at the vet's for days; her liver had stopped working and finally they'd decided the most humane thing to do was to put her to sleep. I drove to my parents' house and the three of us went to the vet's and stood in the room together while he gave her the shot. Susie had been such an important part of the family; we stood right there with her, though it was the sort of thing that no one should have to see.

I held onto my dad and wept, crying harder than I had during any fight my parents and I had during my teen years. Leaving the vet's office that day, I'd experienced one of life's truths that, until encountered firsthand, have all the emotional impact of a math equation: everything dies. The loss of my dog made it clear that I would lose my parents, my friends, my own life someday. In my grief I wondered, as many do, about the point of life and relationships if they all are taken away eventually.

> "The very fact that Susie wagged her tail ferociously at both of us was always a reminder that my mother hadn't suddenly morphed into a controlling, unreasonable being."

The fact that Susie's passing coincided with my moving away made me feel as if I'd officially transitioned into adulthood.

I had finally achieved the maturity to go out into the world, away from the watchful eyes of my parents, but that freedom came at a price. I left home with an awareness that there are losses more profound than the breaches of trust my mother and I had endured.

Even after her death, Susie continued to have an impact on me. For a long time her leash still hung in the stairwell, reminding me whenever I visited home that the time we have with the ones we love is irrecoverably finite. I suspected that aside from the pure loving relationship I'd had with Susie, none of my human interactions would ever be quite that uncomplicated. What mattered wasn't how many times I got hurt or hurt someone else, but how quickly I could achieve forgiveness and appreciate that person for simply being there.

Maggie Flynn is a freelance writer and editor living in Los Angeles. She is currently at work on her first novel.

A Ray of Dogshine

Samantha Ducloux Waltz

"You have to take Isabelle, Mama. You love Golden Retrievers, and she needs us. She's been beaten."

"Sorry, Sweetie. I can't do it."

I straightened the compositions on my desk at the high school where I taught and steeled my resolve. My heart went out to my tender-hearted daughter on the other end of the phone and the puppy in need of a home, but someone had recently beaten our family, too, in a different way. A month earlier, my seventeen-year old son, Ben, had been injured in a horrific automobile accident. Bones in both legs were smashed from ankle to knee, and he had suffered nerve and tissue damage beyond repair. The doctor warned us my son could lose his legs. I slogged through the last month of school, and at home tried to manage our household with the help of a cousin temporarily staying with us. Tami, twenty-one, pitched in when able, as did Joel, my fifteen year-old. Still, every night I dropped into bed exhausted, and then lay awake worrying about Ben.

"If we don't take Isabelle, she'll go to the pound," Tami pleaded.

The thought of a dog going to the pound knotted my stomach. Still, I resisted.

"Ben wants her."

Isabelle

She'd found my jugular.

By the time I got home, fifty pounds of honey-colored fur bounced happily from Tami, to Joel, to Ben in his wheelchair. "So you're Isabelle," I said, scratching her downy tummy and the spot between her ears. Despite her history, she teemed with enthusiasm and good will. Within days she had lifted all our spirits. She brought a ray of "dogshine" into our home that sliced through any gloom.

Some afternoons after school, Joel and I took Isabelle to a small lake at a nearby park where Joel could roller-blade while I jogged. She trotted by his side as he skated around the lake, her tongue lolling, her tail a golden flag. Evenings Tami and I often took her for walks. As soon as we started out, Isabelle would turn her head to catch a loop of the leash in her mouth, appearing to take herself for a walk as she dribbled with excitement.

When I took papers to our deck to grade, Isabelle brought her Frisbee and dropped it at my feet. If I didn't immediately throw it, she'd cock her head at me, then pick it up, carry it to the lawn, toss it in the air herself, whirl and catch it, toss it again, catch it again. When she tired of that game she would climb up the steep hill of cypress, juniper and rhododendrons at the back of our yard, find a straight path between two shrubs, sit on her haunches like a squirrel, and slide down to the lawn, over and over, her mouth open wide in a grin of doggie pleasure.

Best of all, though, was that Ben held Isabelle for long periods of time, stroking her, his face relaxed. She quickly mastered the art of scrambling over the wheel of his wheelchair and settling onto his lap without ever touching his lower legs. Once there, she would twist her head to give him a juicy smooch, and then sit quietly, her front and back legs dangling, until he was ready to shoo her off. He smiled more often, and I credited Isabelle with lifting his spirits.

Summer finally arrived. My cousin returned to Ohio and I planned a family trip to Crater Lake. Ben's legs were healing and the doctor was hopeful he would walk again. Then a bone infection developed in Ben's right calf. A muscle graft to bring blood flow and antibiotics to the site of the infection offered the only hope of saving his leg. A surgeon scraped out the infection, removed one of Ben's abdominal muscles, and wrapped it around his calf. Then he attached veins and arteries to the muscle as well as a graft of skin from Ben's thigh, and finally added antibiotic beads. He then inserted a shunt in a vein near Ben's heart for injection of massive doses of antibiotics. In two weeks, the doctor would remove the bandages. If the leg was pink, Ben would keep it.

That first night after Ben's surgery, I sat on our couch with a magazine in my lap, unable to read a word. Isabelle pushed her nose under my hand so that my fingers found the curve of her head and rested there.

Her soft warmth infused me and I felt a bit stronger. When Ben came home from the hospital, he spent some time with friends who visited, but he spent many hours alone, in bed, his face to the wall, wrestling with inner demons I couldn't even imagine. I felt powerless to help him. Isabelle rested her nose on the bed near his hand should he want to pet her, and I hoped dogs had the healing power I'd heard so much about.

> "Ben wheeled himself to her. 'I know how scary it is,' he whispered into her furry neck, 'but we're both going to get better.'"

One evening, Tami took Isabelle with her on a trip to the store. They drove off together, Tami behind the wheel of her old LeBaron convertible, and Isabelle sitting on her haunches in the passenger seat. Twenty minutes later Tami called, sobbing, from the emergency veterinary clinic. Isabelle had leapt from the car to join some joggers. Miraculously she was still alive. The vet had diagnosed a dislocated hip, but feared internal injuries as well and wanted to keep her overnight. When I hung up the phone, I went to my bedroom and lay face down on the bed. We couldn't lose Isabelle now. Shortly after midnight, unable to sleep, I wandered into the kitchen for a food fix. The kids were all three at the table telling Isabelle stories, so I made hot cocoa for everyone and joined in.

The vet hospital never called with bad news. When Tami brought Isabelle home the next morning, our beloved puppy tried to hobble over to Ben, despite the bandage that helped to stabilize her hip. After just a few steps she sat down with a puzzled look on her face as if to say, "Now why does this hurt so much?" Ben wheeled himself to her. "I know how scary it is," he whispered into her furry neck, "but we're both going to get better."

Isabelle apparently understood his message. She stayed close to Ben as her hip healed, and her dogshine worked right alongside the antibiotics for him. By the time the doctor removed Ben's bandages and found his leg to be a healthy pink, Isabelle was able to join in our shouts and dances of grateful celebration.

Samantha Ducloux Waltz is an award-winning freelance writer who resides in Portland, Oregon. Her essays appear in the *Chicken Soup* series, the *A Cup of Comfort Series*, and numerous other anthologies. She has also written fiction and nonfiction under the names Samellyn Wood and Samantha Ducloux.

Auricle

Carol Murphy

When I am still, with my breathing slowed in meditation, and focus my vision through the glass door, he sometimes appears as a phantom outside my office. An immense dark head with bold friendly eyes staring, pleading to be let inside, just to lie down on his rug, just to be near. Once I even got up, opened the door and looked out into the foggy night, trying to make out his shifting shape moving through the oaks. I am convinced he comes to visit even though I try hard not to think of him too much, because even though I have owned several dogs, tears can still come when I think of Auricle.

He arrived when my daughter was nine and my husband decided we needed another dog. We'd had one when we first got married, one that really became my husband's pet, and when she died he couldn't bring himself to get another. But, fifteen years later, our chronically ill daughter needed a pet, and because she was allergic to just about everything except dogs, we started searching the rescue websites.

We found a good candidate right away. One of the biggest Boxers I have ever seen, he weighed just over 100 pounds. His head was the size of a small sink, and he was a dark brindle color with only a tiny snippet of white, so he at first appeared menacing. Out of the rescue worker's kitchen he slowly maneuvered around smaller dogs, wearing a neck cone to prevent him licking stitches from knee surgery, walked stealthily past my husband, and came over to stand in front of us. We stared at him. He stared back and sniffled ever so slightly.

Auricle

"Wow," said my daughter, and bent forward to kiss him. I pulled her back. "God," I thought. "What if he opens his mouth?" But we were assured he was very gentle, and he was so quiet that we were won over. The rescue worker said that the boxer had been found on the side of a busy county road. She thought that he had either jumped or fallen out of a truck, or been left behind. The unanswered questions only made him dearer.

We named him Auricle because he had an ear that was a little bent, and later we realized how appropriate the name was because of his great heart. I took him for long daily walks, feeling invincible, but I worried a bit because he wanted to look in the back of every truck for something I didn't see, pulling me so hard I eventually had to get a choke chain—but even that was almost useless. With my daughter, he could shrink as if he wanted to be her size, even though he could sprawl out next to her and stretch out so long he would actually become almost twice her size. He was so quiet in the house that often I would turn and he would just be standing there, watching. This was a little spooky at first, but endearing later, as if he were just checking on me, making sure I was safe. He would stare a minute, then move his nose just slightly up, sniff as if he was going to start whining, and then walk back to his bed.

Outside he could run like a deer, fetch anything that was thrown, and leap so high it was sheer joy just to watch him. My son sometimes took him when he played on the local golf course. He was worried at first about Auricle chasing golf balls, but all he had to do was say "no" once and Auricle never touched one. I still don't understand how he knew and obeyed every command as if he had already been trained.

Auricle liked my husband and was happy to see him, but with me or my daughter, he would melt into squiggles so profound I was almost tempted several times to go away and come back just to be so greeted, especially on a bad hair day. Auricle really became my dog. I took him everywhere in my Suburban. He usually stayed in the very back of the car, elongating himself on the rear seat, but when the car was grinding slowly in traffic, he would come and put his head on my shoulder. Or, he'd come very close and sniff just as he did in the kitchen, then go to the back of the car again.

> "A pony came untied, dragging her reins around in the chaos. Auricle calmly followed her, picked up the reins in his mouth and led the pony back to its trailer."

Observation led me to conclude that Auricle had probably been trained as a guard dog. Not the kind that is posted behind chain link fences and barks ferociously when people walk by, but a silent stealth that only springs to life when necessary. Every night he walked the perimeter of the yard before his outhouse duties. He came to the door whenever the doorbell rang or someone knocked, but he never barked. In fact, at first I was worried that he couldn't bark and took him to the vet after owning him for several weeks, but the first thing he did when he saw a little rat terrier in the vet's office was bark.

Auricle could also be counted upon to take care of things of which he was put in charge. I could say, "Watch the car" if I made a short errand, and he would come from the very rear of the Suburban, sit in the passenger's front seat, stay there until I came back, and then, as if on cue, go to the back to lie down. Or, at horse shows, I could say, "Watch the trailer," and he would sit beside it until I came back, sometimes over an hour later. Many times I even left him with a pony, saying only, "Watch the pony." Once, at a horseshow a pony came untied, dragging her reins around in the chaos. Auricle calmly followed her, picked up the reins in his mouth and led the pony back to its trailer.

Auricle was so sensitive that he seemed to fit himself to any situation. This sensitivity appeared to eerily increase when he lost his hearing as he got older. I began using hand signals with him, and he instantly obeyed as if he had been trained to do so as a puppy. I would just motion for him to back up, move forward or sideways, and he would. I could point to his dog bed and he would go lie down. We had become partners, instantly communicating with looks, sniffles, hand movements and gestures.

I have worked with children who rarely spoke or who communicated with great difficulty and Auricle became my therapy dog. I took him to preschools and, with no formal training, he knew to stand quietly amid a bubbling brew of children, allowing each one to touch his huge face. Uncommunicative children who came to my office would first talk to Auricle, and then later sit and serenely pet him, telling me all kinds of stories, their language emerging with each stroke on his long back. He looked like he was sleeping, but always got up and walked each one to the door when they left. Auricle knew his job.

Auricle transformed our lives and the lives of the many children whose hearts he touched and whom he inspired to come out of their shells. It was terrible to lose him. One Saturday, my husband took the Suburban to run some errands. I can picture Auricle now, looking out the window as his truck was driving off, and dashing through the screen door thinking it was me, his constant companion. My husband found him on the road when he came back home. Auricle must have run after that truck until his heart burst. Maybe he thought another truck, with someone else he loved inside, was leaving him behind again. Maybe that is why he keeps visiting, checking to make sure I am still here. I want to tell him that I never left him, but maybe he already knows.

Carol Murphy is a licensed pediatric speech-language pathologist in private practice who has written about children and animals for several years. She has owned about twenty dogs, sometimes two at a time, and can't really remember a life without animals.

Faith

H. Rachelle Graham

I was eighteen years old when I first tried to kill myself. I took a bottle of Zypreza and ended up in my first of many hospital stays. Over the next seven years, I was diagnosed with various mental illnesses, including bipolar disorder, anxiety and schizophrenia. Those years were the roughest time in my life, during which I received of multiple rounds of electroconvulsive treatments, cognitive therapy and heavy doses of many different medications.

My best friend has changed my life, though. She is no ordinary friend. She is a small dog with enormous, black floppy ears that are larger than her face. She has huge brown eyes that open up wide when she is curious or on guard. Most importantly, she is on my side twenty-four hours a day and is one of my strongest defenses against suicidal thoughts and loneliness. Having her around changes everything for me. If I have to go somewhere without her for more than an hour, the depression and anxiety return. When I come back home, she immediately chases my negative thoughts away and I instantly feel better.

Things were very different before she came into my life. Five years ago, my dad came home from his job as a city planner. He saw me in my usual condition, sitting on our black leather couch in my long lavender robe, furry slippers and unkempt hair, watching television. He asked me how I was feeling. I fell on the floor and made a loud moaning sound in response.

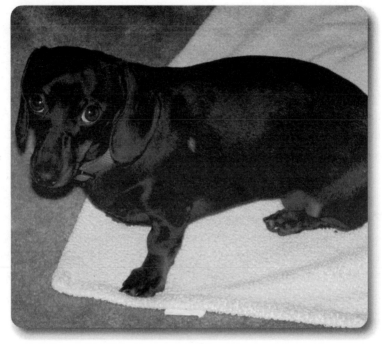

Faith

"You need to get out of the house," he said, looking at me with concern. "Why didn't you go to Pathways today?" Pathways is an adult treatment center for the severely mentally ill where I have attended therapy and activity groups.

"Some of the people there make me nervous."

"Everyone makes you nervous," he said. He was right. I had always been very uncomfortable around people, and was even semi-mute as a child. Now I was in a very bad way mentally, and felt as if there was a hole in my heart that no one and nothing could fill. I was lost, and felt so alone.

The next morning I met my friend Traci for coffee. Afterwards we headed to her place where we were greeted by her dog Sally, a Sheltie with beautiful fluffy hair and an intelligent expression. Sally picked up a ball and begged us to play catch. I played with her for at least an hour while Traci watched television.

After a few more visits, Traci accused me of caring more about the dog than about her. It wasn't quite true! But Sally had begun to fill that hole in my heart. I never felt awkward around her, the way I always had around people. I felt content and able to talk freely for the first time in my life. I longed for the rare times that Traci would go to the store without me or let me take Sally on a walk. When Traci had to take an extended trip and asked me to take care of her dog, I was thrilled. Even though Tracie gave me her house key, I drove Sally to my home. I talked to her on the way home while she barked at passing cars, and I was still talking to her as I parked the car and walked with her to into the house.

"What?" my dad called from inside.

"I'm not talking to you," I said, setting my purse and keys down on the kitchen counter.

"Oh," he said, turning back to his computer. Then he spied Sally and did a double-take. He told me she couldn't stay in the house, even when I pleaded like a five year-old. I had to take her to the garage, and of course I decided to stay there with her. We played catch with one of Dad's old shoes and then we sat side by side under a blanket. I told her all about my day, and she seemed to listen intently. My mom came home and found the two of us sitting in the garage.

"Why are you out here?"

I picked up the dog to show her. Mom smiled. "Oh, come on in. I'll talk to your father. She seems like a good dog."

Between Mom, Sally and me, Dad was overruled. Sally grew on him because she was so well behaved, spending most of her time sitting in the same corner of the house, minding her own business. I often sat with her on the floor.

After having her for a few months, I called the Delta Society and asked if I could get Sally registered as a service dog: they let me know that I could get a temporary service dog vest if I could provide a note from my doctor stating that I had a debilitating medical condition. As soon as I got the vest, I brought Sally to Pathways. I was flattered when so many people talked to me about her. They told me Sally was cute and I said to them, "She knows it." I ended up enjoying my day and for once I was not nervous to be around people.

> "She never judges and only listens... I am able to function with her by my side."

I started going to Pathways every day and looked forward to having Sally by my side. The therapy and activity groups improved my mood so much that I was able to go back to college and finish my degree. I also began writing for local newspapers. I had Sally for a year and loved every minute of it.

But when the time came to give Sally back, I had a mental breakdown. The first few days, I couldn't stop thinking about suicide. My parents were concerned that I was falling back into depression, so Dad decided I could have another dog. The next morning, I pulled myself up off the floor and rinsed my teary face. I drove until I noticed a local pet store with a pink dinosaur out front. I parked and headed in. There I saw three puppies sitting in their cages. I asked the clerk if I could hold the cutest one, a black miniature Dachshund. I hugged her tight while I told the clerk all about how I lost my other dog to her previous owner. He said he had never seen this puppy go to anyone without growling. I returned to the store four more times that day. On the final visit, I brought my mom and my niece and I left with the dog.

Our first night together we chased each other around the house. She stayed up all night and kept me awake, but I didn't mind. I felt content and at peace with my new dog. She became my baby and my new best friend.

She helped me get me through the loss of Sally. She is being trained at Gateway to Canine Partnership to be my service dog. I bring her everywhere and talk to her constantly. I look forward to getting up every morning to rub her tummy and receive her kisses. I am able to function with her by my side. She is my little piece of heaven and that is why I named her Faith.

I have remained in recovery for five years, with no hospital stays. I will always be on medications, but my therapist and I are considering ending therapy in the next few months. I owe a big part of my recovery to Sally and Faith: not just my best dog friends, but my best friends, period.

H. Rachelle Graham earned a Bachelor's degree in journalism and is currently working on a second degree in English at the University of Utah. She has worked for local newspapers including *The Salt Lake Tribune* and *Magna Times* and has had several articles published in magazines including *True Love* and *True Story*. For more on the Delta Society please visit www.deltasociety.org.

Dog Math: Lessons from Abby and Floyde

Melanie Johnston

I've heard a lot of complaints about walking the dogs, mostly from my children. You know, "Awww, Mom, do I have to?" I've heard it from adults too. "I've got to go. Gotta walk the DD." (Dang Dog—an old college friend says this. Did we graduate that long ago that we use the word "dang"?)

I'm not innocent. Sometimes I tire out when it comes to walking them—when it's raining, my back is moaning and I'm waiting, bag in hand, to scoop up their waste from a neighbor's yard. My face is clearly saying, "Ugh." I'm doing my duty.

Yet, when I think about it statistically, my mindset changes. Most days, I walk the dogs a good mile or two or three. Calculating an average, I walk the dogs 48 weeks a year, 5 out of 7 days, minimally 1 mile a day. Doing the math, which I don't like to do, it comes out to 250 miles a year. That's the minimum. If I swing the numbers to the maximum, (which is more realistic) I walk roughly 500 miles a year because of the dogs— more than I would ever do of my own volition. That keeps the waistline down, the cholesterol in check, the stress in a manageable place.

But, you say, what about those rainy, nasty days? Those days you confess that you dread it? Yeah, they're nasty, but the fog in the head clears, regardless. I'd say I have six weeks a year that are wetter than

Abby and Floyde

wet, my feet are cold and the dogs reek of a musky odor that causes our home to smell like a creepy, haunted house. I notice my husband quietly pulling out candles to change the odor dynamic. Yet, odor eaters notwithstanding, when I'm in our cozy kitchen, warm in candlelight, I'm grateful I made it out for some fresh air and logged a couple of miles. My head is clear when our teenagers roar in with unexpected challenges.

The math is difficult to ignore. The way it adds up, through my canines' cavorting, I have come to meet dozens of friends and neighbors that I would never have known otherwise: from London, from India, from China, from Indiana, from the house right next door.

While conversing with one neighbor born in the UK, I helped launch a charity to support a Kenyan orphanage while we watched our fun-loving canines chase a tennis ball. It would never have happened without the tail waggers.

Okay, you say, that's one incident for say, 365 dog walks a year? Because of my two furry best friends, I was drafted by a number of dog lovers to write a pet column for the local paper covering animal issues. From that platform, I was able to persuade the City Public Works Department to exchange typical plastic doggy bags to biodegradable doggy bags in the dog parks. I'm now lobbying them to clean up polluted Bushy Dell Creek, which crawls through the center of town where dogs not only pause to drink but kids often play. Would I have paid attention without our two dogs? I wouldn't count on it.

I saved a cat's life on one of my walks. I saved a dog's life on another. How much does that mean to me? It may sound silly, but I can't calculate it.

I have been given huge hugs by various strangers saying that I prolonged their dog's life because of a column I wrote about toxins like garlic, grapes, raisins, chocolate and onions that can kill a canine or feline.

> "My daily walk of 30 to 60 minutes has opened a tiny view of God's world."

Not to forget the countless small children that have approached me to pet the dogs. What a gift those conversations have been.

"Can I pet your pug?"

"Sure, she loves to be petted."

"I'm five. I have a twin."

"Wow. What's that like?"

"Mostly okay."

Even strange random acts have occurred. The dogs have inspired me to take them to visit the elderly at an assisted living home. And to write a novel based on the many lessons I've learned by watching their constant display of unconditional love. Josh Grogan, author of *Marley & Me*, said to me last fall, "Whatever you do keep going, keep writing. Just don't stop." That wouldn't have happened without Floyde the Pug and Abby the Bernese Mountain Dog.

In fact, just when I was beginning to worry about my high school daughter for no real reason other than a mother's upset stomach, I ran into whom? Her high school counselor. Where? On my dog walk. And? He reassured me that things were going well. My stomach was only in need of Pepto-Bismol, not better grades. But the conversation we had would never have taken place except for the presence of the curious dogs in the midst of a grove of Eucalyptus trees.

Best of all, the walks have given me a space that I would never have created for myself: a green canopy of trees, birds and time that I would not have stumbled upon. My daily walk of 30 to 60 minutes has opened a tiny view of God's world that I couldn't justify visiting virtually every day. I'm not sure I would ever have found it. There are subtle shades of nature I would have missed simply because I wasn't out as often: a morning dove's nest chock full of chicks; a hidden glade of wild cherry trees that blossom from buds into flowers like a dance at cotillion; a regal Golden Eagle floating in the sky above us, her nest nestled in a sugar pine; spooky caves tucked magically into thick Manzanita brush; dozens of wild brown bunnies that hop out at twilight. The dogs have uncovered complicated labyrinths hidden on plateaus in the San Francisco Bay hills, seals camouflaged on the beach, even rare, teeming waterfalls. I can't fathom how much I would have missed without them.

Even last summer, when I lay in the I.C.U. unit at Alta Bates Hospital, my daughter and Floyde snuck into my bed. The three of us fell asleep, tubes surrounding me, beepers beeping in the distance, giving me a chance to feel they safety I longed for, inspiriting my climb back to good health, making even the doctors laugh.

So when I do the math, I am thankful for the chore. I am thankful for the reason to walk that walk every day, log those miles wherever they take me, picking up waste in biodegradable bags, petting soft, happy heads, watching tails wag, even in the rain, fog or when I have a runny nose. The numbers add up.

Melanie Johnston is the author of *What My Father Saw*, a book about her father's experience as one of the liberators of the concentration camp at Buchenwald. She lives in Piedmont, California, where she writes a dog column for the *Piedmont Post* called *Dear Abby, the Bernese Mountain Dog*.

A Dog with Two Tails

Celeste de Mazia

"Hi Gran," said Emma, bouncing in through my office door with her usual impish grin and picking up the folder on my desk. "How's everyone today?"

"Well, Sally is still very down."

I passed Emma the case notes on our latest resident at Fernleas: *Sally Morrison, aged 70, widowed 6 months ago. Family: 1 daughter & grandchild living in Australia. General physical health quite good, apart from mild osteo-arthritis and tendency to respiratory problems.* No doubt the latter was exacerbated by her forty-a-day smoking habit. As the retired landlady of an East End pub, Sally liked her daily tipple as well. From what we had gathered, she'd been quite a lively character, life and soul of the party. This grieving role did not sit well with her. She just seemed to be giving up. It didn't help matters that she had a secret store of vodka hidden under the bed. She wouldn't eat much at all, and refused to mix with the other residents. I tried to persuade her to spend some time out of her room with musical evenings, TV suppers and theater outings, to no avail.

With a faraway look in her eyes, Emma said that Sally's problems reminded her of a dog that had been brought to the shelter where she works as a volunteer, a dear little cocker spaniel. "She was just left on the doorstep," Emma said. "Apparently the owners are emigrating, but you'd think they would have at least found her a proper home, wouldn't you?"

Jessie

Emma sighed, looking deflated. "Her collar tag says Jessie. She won't settle down, refuses her food and just wants to be on her own. She's wary of the other dogs; sudden noises unsettle her, and she's obviously pining. At night, she lies there whining and whimpering. It's starting to get to me, Gran."

"Try not to worry too much, pet," I reassured her. "Animals are amazingly resilient, and so are people." Emma smiled appreciatively, took the other residents' case notes and began her morning rounds. After she left, Sally's dilemma preyed on my mind. It was also causing a feeling of restlessness and tension amongst the residents—almost as if we were all waiting for something to happen. On the rare occasions that

Sally said anything, her language could be pretty colourful: a true Eastender! She'd managed to upset Sheila, who did the cooking, as well as one of the agency staff, who'd walked out in a huff. I knew something had to be done with the feisty widow, but what?

It wasn't until later that evening that the germ of an idea began to present itself. By the time I was ready for bed, I'd convinced myself it might just work. I knew I could rely on Emma's cooperation, so I made the call. Next morning, Emma arrived with Jessie in tow. The only problem seemed to be Jessie's reluctance to meet anyone, let alone Sally. She cowered under the table in the conservatory, shivering. We all took turns offering her tasty morsels, water, even a bone to chew on. I looked at Jessie with growing exasperation.

> "C'mon, yer silly mutt. You an' me, we're gettin' outta this bloomin' place!"

"How can we tempt her to come out before Sally is down for her coffee?"

Emma said, "Well, she is a rescue dog, Gran, so she doesn't trust easily. Maybe we should just allow things to take their course." Emma wandered over to chat to Sheila, and they were soon absorbed in planning recipes for the week.

As I busied myself with the lunchtime routine, the usual hustle and bustle of Fernleas took over, and we all forgot Jessie, who seemed content to lie under the table, occasionally licking her paws and gazing at us with her soulful brown eyes. It wasn't until I emerged from a mound of paperwork, at around 3:30, that I remembered her.

Just then, Emma appeared at the door. She beckoned me towards the conservatory, finger to her lips. We approached the conservatory and stood in a corner to see ornery old Sally coaxing Jessie out from under the table. And it was working!

"C'mon, yer silly mutt. You an' me, we're gettin' outta this bloomin' place." As the spaniel, normally so timid, looked up at her trustingly,

Sally chuckled. "That's the ticket. Can't 'ide away no more, can we? Yeah, and we told Emma we was goin' walkies, didn't we?" Sally spoke soothingly as she deftly clipped the lead onto Jessie's collar. "There yer go, a nice li'l walkies down to our local. That'll set us both to rights, my littl'un. Let's go show 'em 'ow it's done."

Emma and I muffled our laughter with some difficulty. I had the distinct feeling the whole performance had been for our benefit. But I didn't care. As long as Sally and Jessie were happy, so was I. Not to mention my granddaughter, Emma.

The next day, I received a text message from her: "NICE 1 GRAN" and an image of a dog with two wagging tails.

Celeste de Mazia lives on the south coast of England with her husband and for the past 20 years her work as a mentor/astrologer has inspired her to write articles on self-development, healing, and the esoteric. She is a published poet and is currently writing short stories.

Spirit of Adventure

Glynis Scrivens

At the end of 1992, I came down with a serious chronic illness. It was a time of great fear and uncertainty, and not just because of my health. My family's home had been burgled five times over a period of seven years. It was a constant worry, especially after I interrupted one burglar as he was using our phone to call a taxi; he had packed our valuables into two boxes and was about to head off. On another occasion, a burglar tried to set fire to the house.

We'd been discussing the idea of getting a dog, preferably a male. At the same time our son was entering adolescence and we felt that the right kind of dog would help steady him on his journey through high school and into adulthood. He had two sisters but pined for male company. I had reservations about getting a puppy; I'd seen friends have their good shoes chewed up and the impact on their gardens of a bored pup with too much time on his paws. Could we handle all that extra stress? And then there was the issue of compatibility. Some dogs just didn't suit some owners. "If only there was some way of road testing a dog," I said to my husband. "Get to know one before deciding whether or not to keep him."

There was a way, as it turned out, because a friendly mutt was about to road test us. We were holidaying at the beach and he found us almost as soon as we arrived. For the whole week we were there, this black and white rascal was on his best behavior, playing with the children all day,

Spirit

and sleeping on the veranda every night. He even allowed three year-old Amy to put a towel on his back and ride him around the garden. We were able to enjoy all the pleasures of pet ownership with none of the responsibilities. Spirit, as we called him, went for walks along the beach with the children, played ball, learned how to play hide and seek and generally had a great holiday, too.

When it was time for us to pack up and go home, we started to wonder who he belonged to. All week we'd just assumed he lived somewhere on the same street where we were holidaying, but now we began to feel uneasy. After all, we were the only ones who'd been feeding him and putting out bowls of water. What would become of him when we left? We'd learned to care enough about him to worry about his welfare.

Thanks to the tag attached to his collar, we were able to track down his address: two miles away on the other side of the highway. By this time, the prospect of parting with him was becoming increasingly difficult. The children were crying about it, so we decided to ask his owner if we could buy him. But Derek, the owner, was over the moon to hear we had Spirit. "I've been looking for him all week. Thank heavens he's safe. I'll be right over." Ten minutes later, an old truck pulled up outside and a tradesman climbed out. He was wearing old paint-stained blue shorts, and a rough dark blue cotton shirt. He looked tired—until he caught sight of the black and white dog that hurtled towards him.

Witnessing the rapturous response from Spirit when he saw his owner left us feeling empty. His whole body wriggled with pleasure. For us, though, it was hard to face the reality of going home without our new friend. Spurred on by lots of looks from the children, we suggested we could look after him, but as expected our offer was politely brushed aside as unthinkable. Who could blame him? Derek had chosen this dog when he was just an hour old, unable to resist the pup among the litter who was showing the most spirit. They'd been best friends for the past eighteen months.

It seemed as though nature was mimicking the atmosphere inside our rented house that night when a fierce thunderstorm struck. It poured rain. We couldn't sleep for the lightning, and the hail on the tin roof sounded like bullets. The storm raged without cease, making sleep impossible. At half past one, we heard a familiar thump outside on the veranda. Running over to the window, I could just make out two white and black spotted paws stretched out in their usual position.

Spirit was drenched, hungry, tired and ecstatic to see us again. Hugging him in the rain, we quickly put together a supper of Weetbix and milk for him, made a pot for tea for ourselves, and resolved to ask again about keeping him. After all, he'd made the same decision, as far as we were concerned, by venturing out into the storm and crossing the highway to find us again. We were tempted to simply disappear with him the next morning, but decided to do the right thing.

Our honesty was unexpectedly rewarded. The next morning, the dog's owner was offered a position he couldn't turn down. A dream job, with just the one snag. It was in North Queensland, and he had been advised that he wouldn't be able to bring any pets with him. Spirit was ours!

In the early years of my illness, I was often housebound. Spirit brought the world to me and kept a smile on my face. He'd beg dinners from passersby, and we'd find him tucking into a takeaway container of Chinese food or some fish and chips. One morning he was discovered dining on oysters, with half a bottle of chardonnay beside him. We suspected he'd stolen these, but who knows? He made us happy, and truly became a member of the family.

> "Fear left when Spirit arrived."

And, importantly, I've always felt completely safe with him around. My illness used to make me feel terribly vulnerable, but Spirit has been a wonderful antidote. Nobody has entered our home without Spirit's permission. Or left. He doesn't bark at people. He simply watches them. If he thinks they're up to no good, he positions himself quietly between them and the gate. One day, when I was very ill, a man came to the door, offering to replace the roof. There'd been warnings of a roofing scam in the local papers, so I was on my guard. The man was 6'6" and solidly built. I told him I wasn't interested. As he turned to leave, I saw him falter. His voice shook. "I can't go. Your dog is in my way." I whistled, and Spirit stood aside. It was an empowering experience.

On another occasion, when the children were very young, we watched in alarm as a man took his trousers off and put them into our wheelie bin on our footpath. He then walked into our garden and up to the front door wearing nothing but a small grey nappy. Perhaps he was a harmless homeless man, but how could I take any chances? It was only a couple of weeks ago that a man meeting this description had burned down a house in our suburb. I phoned the police, locked the house, and kept Spirit with me till they arrived to escort the intruder away.

Spirit has made the difference between my coping and not coping. His silent strength is contagious, and I've always known he will protect us from whatever risk we face. It's been very difficult to bring up children while suffering poor health. Spirit has eased my load by defusing many difficult situations, from protecting us from intruders to devouring spiders. With him by my side, I keep my doors open to let in sunshine and life. Fear left when Spirit arrived.

Spirit has been with us 15 years now, and his whiskers are tinged with grey. But he has always been there for us, throwing himself in the path of any danger that might beset us. His spirit of adventure has kept me safe and sane through these years, providing me with many happy anecdotes and memories.

Glynis Scrivens lives in Brisbane, Australia with her husband, three children, and a menagerie of pets: hens, guinea pigs, two dogs, a rainbow lorikeet and goldfish. She writes fiction for women's magazines and is a regular contributor to *Writers' Forum* magazine.

The Baby

Stephanie R. Snowe

Everything was finally perfect. After a failed marriage, I had the husband of my dreams. We owned a little house. We both had good jobs. The twins I had during my first marriage were thriving.

Everything was exactly what it should be. The time was right for my husband and me to have a child. At last, it seemed I would achieve my dearest dream of a complete, happy family. There was just one problem. I couldn't get pregnant. In frustration I went to my doctor, who ran a battery of tests. He ended up giving me the sad news: I was infertile. I was utterly heartbroken, and also terribly angry. My husband wanted to help me, but we disagreed on how to handle the news. I thought that we should do everything in our power, spend every dime we had, to ensure that somehow, some way, I would be able to have a baby. He wanted to get a dog.

I balked. I loved dogs, but I just didn't see how a dog could be an appropriate substitute for a baby. How could an animal assuage the deep pain and loss I felt as a woman, or defuse the anger and frustration that had come to dominate my emotions? We fought several times over the issue until I at last gave in.

Shortly thereafter, we adopted a small brown pup with a fluffy tail. Ginger was so small then, only nine pounds. I picked her up and was amazed at how light she was. I held her all the way home, swaddled in

Ginger

a baby blanket. I *might as well get good use out of these blankets,* I thought, bitterly. Ginger responded to my angry musing by leaning up thoughtfully and licking me on the nose. Ginger settled into our home as though she had always been there.

Even though she was a very nice dog, I still wasn't sure she could ever fill the void left by my inability to have another child. Around this time, my father became ill with cancer. I was afraid he might die, so I packed my car with my twins and the little puppy dog, and drove five hundred miles to see him after his first surgery. On the way back home from this emergency visit, we were driving through the Blue Ridge Mountains. My little children were asleep. I began to cry. For my dad and all of his struggles. For my failings as a woman, and as a wife. For the baby I would never bear, give birth to, hold, watch grow. The child that simply would never exist. I was overwhelmed by a sense of loss.

As I wept, Ginger crawled between the center console and the driver's seat, and laid her head on my shoulder, looking at me with her big brown eyes as though to say, "It will be okay."

> "I still wasn't sure she could ever fill the void left by my inability to have another child."

Eventually, the tears stopped flowing, and by the time I got back home I realized that a great deal of my heartache had been left somewhere behind. Ginger's unquestioning love had truly chased the clouds from my heart.

Ginger is two years old now. She is not just our pet; she is most decidedly a part of our family. Every December we have a birthday party for her. Far from being baby sized, she's sixty-six pounds now, with long orangey-brown hair and a sweet, loving temperament. Every time she sees us she is overcome with joy, and so are we. She loves every single one of us unconditionally.

And she never, ever has a stinky diaper.

Stephanie Snowe lives in East Tennessee with her husband, twin son/daughter and Ginger. Her first book, *Meeting Mr. Wrong: The Romantic Misadventures of a Southern Belle*, was published in February, 2009.

My Heroic Dog

Suzan L. Wiener

My husband Howard talked about getting a dog, but my allergies stopped us from becoming pet owners. I liked animals, but I experienced long sneezing fits when I was near one. One rainy afternoon, however, a pet found us, and we were very lucky that she did. Because she went on to save Howard's life, literally.

Hearing yelping at our door, I saw one of the most forlorn dogs. I felt so sorry for her that I quickly let her come in. Though her black fur was drenched and matted, I could still see she was beautiful. I gave her food and water and waited for the sneezing to start, which it did.

Oblivious to my plight, our guest made herself comfortable. Howard wanted to adopt her, but I didn't want to spend the rest of my life sneezing. We compromised and agreed to keep her while we ran a notice in the local paper. No one claimed her. Howard was ecstatic, and truthfully, so was I. That sweet dog became entwined in our lives. We named her Midnight. From the onset, Midnight seemed to favor Howard and loved to sit at his feet or accompany him in the back yard while he puttered in his garden.

Bright and early one Saturday morning, Howard went out to the back yard to plant some tomatoes. Midnight followed closely behind. I was in the kitchen washing dishes when I heard a commotion. I threw open the back door and to my horror, saw the neighbor's pit bull charging toward Howard, who is unable to move quickly because of his bad

Midnight

back. There was no time for me to react; fortunately I didn't have to. Midnight sprang to Howard's defense, barking and looking menacing. It was an uneven contest, our Midnight against this powerful pit bull. But the only thing that mattered to Midnight was to protect her family. The other dog ran away, whimpering.

That night, Midnight was treated to plenty of petting and the most expensive gourmet dog food we could find. Howard made a medal for her that read, "The Bravest Dog in the World" and placed it around her neck.

I'm not sure Midnight understood why she was receiving so much attention, but she seemed to enjoy it. Midnight had been Howard's dog, but that Saturday she became my dog too. Despite the allergy shots, we both love Midnight. Midnight's only problem is deciding whom she loves best.

Suzan L. Wiener has had many stories, poems and articles published in periodicals including *Mature Living, Mature Years, MetroSeven* (Australia), *FellowScript, Cross & Quill, Verses, Complete Woman* and *Woman's Day*.

Healing Together

A.R. Darke

I watched with a smile as my ten year-old limped eagerly into the living room. His knees had once again swollen and locked in a bent position. Movement was painful for him during an arthritis flare-up, and normally he would have stayed in bed until it passed. Today, however, was a very special day. Today young Mark was getting his first puppy.

He had wanted a dog for so long, and in the past I had always been reluctant. A puppy meant work, and I was swamped. Also, this type of animal would need exercise. Mark couldn't run and play with it. He would only be able to go for short, slow walks on good days. In my opinion a cat or a fish would have been a much better pet for him.

Then it happened. My sister-in-law decided to get a Great Pyrenees puppy. I agreed to accompany her to pick it out. I had no intention of bringing one home myself, but when we arrived at the house my heart sank into my stomach. The litter had been an accident, and the people had not been caring for the pups at all. They were starving and full of parasites. Only two remained alive in the barn. Sis took the female while I crouched on the floor gazing at the male lying in the hay. His sad eyes seemed to call out to me. He tried to walk over, but stumbled and fell. I scooped him into my arms and returned to the car. I couldn't just leave him there. He needed a home. He needed my home.

I phoned ahead to tell my husband to meet me outside with a basket. He sighed heavily when I told him what I had done. A Great Pyrenees is a very large dog, he pointed out. What would we do with it? I said that we would figure that out, but the pup was staying no matter what. Mark wanted a dog, and this little guy was the one for him. Something in my gut told me I was doing the right thing.

The boy took a seat on the sofa. He was looking around wildly for the puppy. My husband had already told him that I was bringing one home. "Where's my puppy?" he asked. I smiled and pulled the little ball of fluff from the basket where he had curled up under a blanket. I placed him gently on Mark's lap. The child threw his arms around him in a tight hug. "Be careful with him. He's not in very good shape. He has worms, so don't let him lick your face. He has a vet appointment the day after tomorrow. It was the best I could get."

For the first time in a long time I saw a sparkle in my son's eyes. His pain had been forgotten. He had a dog, and he was happy. I had made the right choice. They slept in bed together that night. It was picture perfect. Mark talked to the pup like a new friend. He named the dog Stryker, after a character in a book. He had researched the breed online, and learned how to best take care of his new pet. The boy wanted to be a responsible owner, and was looking forward to proving that he could do something productive despite his physical limitations.

> "I saw a sparkle in my son's eyes. His pain had been forgotten."

The next day I was in the kitchen when a scream sounded from the living room. Stryker lay on the floor shaking and foaming at the mouth. Mark was bent over him, crying. The pup was having a seizure. My husband grabbed the phone and called the vet's office. They said to bring him in immediately. We piled into the car and rushed to town.

After some tests we learned that worm larvae had migrated to the puppy's brain, causing an infection and swelling. Dr. Riggs took me into the hall while everyone else waited in the exam room. He closed the door so they couldn't hear.

"This doesn't look good. I won't lie to you. I've never seen one live through this. Normally I encourage the owner to put the animal down."

I was horrified. "I can't do that!"

"You'll be throwing your money away. We're talking about a thousand bucks, maybe more. Besides, even if he lives the infection will leave him brain damaged. You already have a disabled child. Can you take on a disabled dog too?"

"I'll do whatever it takes. Give me the meds. I'm a nurse. If I can treat people, I can treat a sick puppy. Stryker has to live. My son needs him."

We left the office that day with an empty bank account. Mark sat in the back seat with the dog on his lap. I had explained what was wrong, and had even disclosed that the odds were stacked against us.

"Mommy?" The small voice came from behind me. "Please don't let Stryker die."

Back at home Mark rolled out a sleeping bag on the floor of my bedroom. He announced that he would be staying with Stryker at my bedside until he was better. When I went to call him to dinner I found that the room had become a campground. He had moved in clothes, books, and even a folding tray for eating and home schooling. He refused to come out to eat or visit.

Those two weeks of Stryker's illness were the longest of my life. At first things seemed grim, but at last Stryker began to walk around a bit. It was slow going and he fell a lot, but at least he was moving. After fourteen days we received a clean bill of health from the doctor. The brain damage had affected Stryker's ability to walk, but he was alive.

However, our joy was not to last. Six months later brought bad news for Mark. His arthritis flare-ups were becoming more frequent and more painful. His knees and ankles were deteriorating from the disease. The doctor increased his medications. He had to have a procedure to increase the fluid in the joints. Now he had to undergo physical therapy. The doctors prescribed walking every day. How could he do it? Extended walking was hard for him. It hurt, and he would often fall. He hated the way people stared at him as he limped along. The embarrassment kept him in the house most of the time. My heart went out to him.

The morning after I told him about the therapy, he arrived in the kitchen in sweats and sneakers. In his hand he held a leash. "What are you doing?" I asked.

"Stryker and I are going to take our walk," he announced.

"Oh Mark, sweetie, Stryker may not be able to do it."

He shook his head. "I'll help him Mom, and he can help me. We'll do it together."

With that, they were off. I watched from the window as the pair made their way down the sidewalk. Mark's right leg gave and he went down. I started for the door, but I stopped when I saw Stryker move over beside Mark and brace himself. Mark placed his hand firmly on Stryker's back and pushed himself into a standing position. They continued on a couple more steps. Then, it was the dog that wobbled. Mark steadied him and they plodded on. They were helping each other!

It's been over a year since that first outing, and the pair still makes their morning rounds of the neighborhood. Mark is no longer bothered by people's stares. He isn't ashamed anymore of being "different." He has a best friend beside him. It may take them a little longer to get where they're going, and they may stumble along the way, but as long as they have each other they will get there. People said I was crazy for spending all that money on a puppy, but the quality of life he has given my son is worth more than anything I could buy.

A.R. Darke lives in Crossville, Tennessee with her husband, three children, and four dogs. Once in the nursing field, she currently spends her time writing and home schooling her children. She enjoys sewing, art, reading, and writing, and music.

Pee Monster

Ann Hoffman

My roommate and I had both recently become single. She spent her time scheduling dates through various dating websites. I, on the other hand, spent hours and hours on Petfinder.com, wishing I could have a dog. I wanted a dog, but wasn't sure I had the time. So I compromised: I started fostering dogs. It was a perfect situation. All the perks of having a dog, but without the worry of having enough time for it when I got busy with schoolwork or boarding if I wanted to travel.

Of course, each dog was better than the last. All of them were sweet and easy to love. They showed up in the van from the pound, scruffy and dirty. I would race home from school to meet the van, meet the pup, and immediately head to the bathtub with my new buddy. My clean, socialized, and loving fosters never stayed for more than two weeks; it was heartbreaking to see each one go, but worth it in the end.

About two years ago I was fostering my fifth pup. We were walking early in the morning to our local dog run. I didn't live in the best part of town at the time; I was a student at a medical center, and, like most medical centers, it was in a rough neighborhood. Some people fought dogs at the run, some people abandoned dogs there. I think people left their dogs in the run because they couldn't take care of them but didn't want to leave them on the street, and the dog run community (I imagine it's the same everywhere), would never let an abandoned pet go without a home.

Daphne

This morning my foster and I came up to the dog park to find the most recent orphan. She wagged her tail when I unlatched the gate; she almost jumped out of her skin when we walked in. What a lovely puppy. A tag taped to her neck said "Daphne." About fifteen pounds and six months old, the vet said. She had a little cold, maybe from spending the night outside. Maybe more than one night.

She and my foster got along, so she came home with us that morning. I made lost dog flyers; I had the vet check for a microchip. Two weeks passed and I heard nothing. No one from the dog park would have been surprised by this, except for the fact that she was so ridiculously sweet and cute. People stopped me to ask what breed she was; they wanted a dog that looked like her. "Where did you get her? What is she?" they would ask. "Awwwww, did you see that?" they would say. "The cutest dog ever!"

But I knew the ugly truth: this dog was a pee machine. She may have answered to Daphne, but my roommate and I called her Pee Monster. I would take her out for over an hour, she would do her business. We would come in, I would get ready to leave, and she would start to pee. Oceans. Everywhere. I had to start buying bargain paper towels.

My foster dogs all had a few issues here and there, but nothing that wasn't fixed after a few days of loving care. This peeing, on the other hand, went on for months. I tried everything, positive reinforcement, walks every hour, then every half hour. I could have taken Daphne out every minute, but as soon as I would get ready to leave the apartment, she would pee.

I talked to the vet about it. He said it could take months to train her because this puppy was scared to death that I was going to leave her and never come back, to leave her crying, waiting alone for someone to be there when the sun came up the next day. As if I did not spend enough time rushing back and forth from school to make sure my floors stayed as dry as possible!

I tried another technique: leaving the apartment for only five minutes at a time. I would sit in the hallway for five minutes, and come back, leave again for ten minutes, and come back. It took us about a month to work our way up to several hours, and then miraculously, she was housebroken!

She was still the neediest dog I had ever met, but she was now the best dog ever, and after all of this work, she was definitely mine. I gave her more flattering nicknames, like Dapper and D-monster, instead of Pee Monster.

Six months later, I met Jeff. It was amazing. We hit it off immediately. Common interests, lots of energy, a love of dogs. He fell in love with me *and* with Daphne. Within two weeks of meeting we were spending all of our time together; soon we would get a little less sleep to wake up a bit earlier just to spend more time together.

Most importantly, Daphne welcomed him into our lives with open paws (although at the time, she welcomed anyone who would wrestle with her and give her a good belly rub). By this time, Daphne was just eighteen pounds and I could carry her with me around New York City by subway. Like me, she loved shopping and became a real personality at our favorite stores. On the streets she would strut, with her curly tail held high. Not only did she have confidence, she had style.

Jeff would bring lunch to me on many days. He seemed to be the most supportive person in my life. At the time, graduate school was beginning to wear down my confidence and it was great to have someone so close who believed in me. I thrived on his words, and loved how they made me feel.

A few more months passed, and Daphne and I decided that we would move in with Jeff. It seemed perfect. Fast, but perfect. We would live downtown in Greenwich Village, a much nicer part of town. I would have to commute, but Jeff worked close by and could take Daphne out several times during the day. We were going to build a little (I mean seriously tiny) home together in the heart of New York City.

Jeff took me for nice dinners and fun evenings out, and he would bring Daphne new dog treats and toys almost every day. This was too good to be true. In fact, some of my friends said it was dangerously unreal. I assured them that we knew what we were doing and that, if anything, he was more in love with me than I was with him anyway.

It was not long before Jeff and I experienced the first frustrations of putting two lives together in one little apartment. I think the first fight was about me doing his laundry. The second was about my friendship with an old boyfriend. After that, things escalated quickly. I was cleaning the apartment and washing all of our clothes all the time, not going to work until it was done. I often needed to ease his fears that I was not interested in other guys, that I loved him and wouldn't leave him.

On his aunt's birthday, I didn't wash the pants Jeff wanted to wear to her party; I had already missed a day of work to stay home and clean for his friends who were coming over that weekend. He came home before his aunt's birthday dinner and began searched frantically for something to wear. But he wanted to wear *those* pants, and I watched as his frustration grew.

Things began to fly. With a swipe of his arm, my make-up compacts and perfume bottles fell to the floor. I ran to the bathroom in tears. He threw random sports equipment from the bottom of his closet in my direction. I sank to the floor.

Things got worse. I met with a male colleague at a conference, and came home to Jeff calling me unforgivable names. Once he literally kicked me out of bed. I began to resist his demands, and as I showed more resilience, he turned on Daphne. He kicked her out of bed; he slapped her in the face when she would bark. "She has to learn," Jeff said. Apparently, he was trying to teach both us something.

> "I screamed, 'Stop hitting my dog! Do not hit my dog!!'"

She began to pee again. He would yell, and she would pee. When Jeff would find it (for some reason, it was always he who stepped in it), he would yell at me and slap Daphne. I would hold her as I cleaned it up.

One night, he stepped in an accident again. He stomped over to the couch, grabbed Daphne, threw her to the ground in her pee, and began hitting her in the head with his hand. I screamed, "Stop hitting my dog! Do not hit my dog!!" I was so angry. I don't have a quick temper, but I used to have a backbone. In that moment, I felt a sense of self that I had not felt in many months. I didn't need validation from someone like this, and I certainly would not deal with a coward who could take his anger out on a helpless puppy an eighth his size. I had been so too patient and tolerant, and I had put myself and now Daphne in an abusive relationship. *I was in an abusive relationship.*

For someone who had been as confident as I, no one, including myself, could believe it. Daphne and I slept on the couch that night.

For Jeff, things went back to normal quickly. But while he was planning a business trip to Taiwan, I was planning my escape with Daphne to the Upper West Side. Daphne, however, had other plans. She began barking when she heard Jeff coming home. She protected her food from him, growling and snarling if he reached near it. She was aggressive with him and protective of me. She would sleep so close to me that I almost had to pry her off me in the morning. And she had stopped peeing again.

Until one night, when Jeff came home particularly late. We were fast asleep and he was drunk. He picked up Daphne to play with her and passed out, holding her to his chest. Hours later he got up to go to work. "She panted all over me. She must have been hot," he said, when he sluggishly got up. I rolled over to find his soaked t-shirt on the bed. It was absolutely drenched. I touched his shirt, and put my hand up to my nose. Daphne had peed all over him in his sleep!

He left for Taipei a few days later, and while I packed up our things Daphne spent the time peeing on all the clothes Jeff had left on the floor. Her accuracy was astounding. I left his things where they lay and whisked Daphne away to our new, safe, uptown home.

It had been a long first year together. Daphne and I learned a lot. Maybe she did not choose her situation, like I did mine, but we both figured out how to stand up for ourselves. Daphne can still be seen strutting up and down Fifth Avenue visiting her favorite shops, jumping in the fountain at Columbus Circle, and answering her admirers with an adoring look and tail held high.

Anne Hoffman attended the University of California at Berkeley as an undergraduate and Columbia University for her graduate studies. She has been fortunate enough to grow up in a loving and endlessly supportive family. Although her family moved often, she has found good friends everywhere, especially in the dog parks.

The Love of a Dog

Carolyn Johnson Foltyn

True friends love us no matter our economic status, outward beauty or personal circumstances. They are there to pick up the pieces when life treats us unkindly and when our dreams are crushed by the weight of the world, when we are ill or sad or lonely. They are there, too, in times of joy and prosperity, when all is well and when we are blessed with good health and adequate wealth.

Such was the case with one very special Border Collie, Jipp, who was my constant companion, my most adoring fan and my best friend. Jipp was born in 1980 on a small farm in a rural town in Oregon. It is said that beauty is in the eye of the beholder and such was the case with Jipp. He may not have been the poster boy for his breed, nor did he boast of extraordinary lineage but when I laid eyes on him, I knew that destiny had somehow brought us together. I brought Jipp to my home state of California, where he spent the next seven years teaching me the meaning of true friendship, unconditional love and the importance of living life to its fullest.

Jipp was unlike any other puppy I had ever known. Even on the first night away from his mom, he never whined or cried and was very content just to lie near me, stare into my eyes and listen to my voice. Since he accompanied me nearly everywhere I went, Jipp would sit and listen to conversations with family, friends and colleagues. He would look in the eyes of the person speaking and, as many friends observed,

Jipp

he seemed to understand every word he was hearing. Everyone loved him, and this special dog was invited to a variety of functions when no other pets were allowed. His reputation was stellar.

Jipp brought me through a painful divorce. He was always there to comfort me and to provide companionship without judgment. I will always believe that God knew I would need his presence in my life in order to survive such a life-changing and difficult ordeal. Dogs bring out the best in us because they inspire us to look beyond ourselves, to protect the defenseless. In the face of great sorrow—the loss of loved ones, divorce, illness, and financial hardships—our dogs remain our loyal companions. Their devotion is written in their eyes and in their body language and in their intense desire to please us. And for many of us, our lives have been changed immeasurably and forever by the love of a dog.

Carolyn Johnson Foltyn lives in Southern California and is an animal lover and the devoted mother of her very special 9 year-old daughter, Sarah. She is the daughter of Harlan and Arlene, who are her heroes, and the sister of Susan and Dale. Her faith in the Lord is the cornerstone of her life.

Resources

Here you will find information on some of the foremost organizations dedicated to the care and training of dogs for work, companionship and for helping people in need.

American Kennel Club
8051 Arco Corporate Drive, Suite 100
Raleigh, NC 27617-3390
(919) 233-9767
www.akc.org/breeds/rescue.cfm

The American Kennel Club is one of the largest registries of purebred dog pedigrees in the United States. The Kennel Club also promotes events for purebred dogs such as the National Dog Show.

The Monks of New Skete
(518) 677-3928
www.newsketemonks.com/dogs.htm

Locate in the Taconic Mountains of Cambridge, Massachusetts, the monks have written several dog training books including *The Art of Raising a Puppy* and *How to Be Your Dog's Best Friend: Classic Training Manual for Dog Owners*.

Canine Companions for Independence

P.O. Box 446

Santa Rosa, CA 95402-0446

800-572-BARK (2275)

866-CCI-DOGS (224-3647)

www.cci.org/site/c.cdKGIRNqEmG/b.3978475/k.BED8/Home.htm

Canine Companions for Independence is the largest non-profit organization that trains and provides assistance dogs, as well as ongoing support to ensure quality partnerships. All CCI dogs and services are provided free of charge. CCI is funded by private contributions and receives no government funding.

Dog Scouts of America

P.O. Box 158

Harrison, OH 45030

dogscouts@hotmail.com

(513) 505-5071

www.dogscouts.org

Dog Scouts for America is a non-profit organization seeking to improve the relationship between owner's and their dogs, as well as to enrich the life of dogs in general. DSA provides TK, grief counseling when dogs die, and various camps throughout America for both dogs and their owners. With the motto, "Let us learn new things so that we may become more helpful," DSA provides various badges and certificates for dogs.

Guiding Eyes for the Blind

611 Granite Springs Road

Yorktown Heights, NY 10598

(800) 942-0149

(914) 245-4024

www.guidingeyes.org

Located in New York State, Guiding Eyes for the Blind is a non-profit organization that places trained dogs with owners by breeding, raising, and training dogs specifically for the purpose of aiding the blind.

Guide Dogs for the Blind
P.O. Box 151200
San Rafael, California 94915-1200
(800) 295-4050
www.guidedogs.com

Guide Dogs for the Blind is a guide dog school located in the United States with centers primarily located on the West Coast. Guide Dogs for the Blind also provides information and videos for dog owners interested in learning more about the service.

Dogs for Diabetics
Mailing Address
1647 Willow Pass Road #157
Concord, CA 94520-2611

Facility Address
Training Center
1400 Willow Pass Court
Concord, CA 94520
(925) 246-5785
info@dogs4diabetics.com
www.dogs4diabetics.com

Dogs for Diabetics provides trained dogs to detect type 1 diabetes-related hypoglycemia.

The Mixed Breed Dog Clubs of America
13884 State Route 104
Lucasville, OH 45648-8586
(740) 259-3941
Libi-Lew@juno.com
www.mbdca.tripod.com

The Mixed Breed Dog Clubs of America (MBDCA) is a registry for spayed or neutered mixed-breed dogs. Stressing obedience and companionship, MBDCA is the only dog organization in America that requires a conformation dog to obtain an obedience degree before he/she competes for titles in obedience, tracking, etc.

Paws With A Cause
4646 South Division
Wayland, MI 49348
(800) 253-7297
www.pawswithacause.org

Paws With A Cause is a non-profit organization that trains assistance dogs for people with disabilities, many of which are obtained through rescue endeavors.

Project POOCH
P.O. Box 305
Lake Oswego, OR, 97034
Phone: (503) 697-0623
Fax: (503) 636-5908
http://www.pooch.org/

Positive Opportunities, Obvious Change with Hounds is a non-profit organization that aims to rehabilitate incarcerated youths by actively training difficult-to-adopt dogs. By practicing the principles of positive reinforcement and behavior modification to manage the behavior of the dogs, trainers learn how to successfully manage their own behavior.

The Seeing Dogs Alliance
116 Potters Lane
Send, Woking, GU23 7AL
www.seeingdogs.org.uk

The Seeing Dogs Alliance (SDA) is an alliance of guiding dog owners, working to improve conditions of Seeing Eye dogs and their owners. Primarily based in the U.K., the SDA is one of the only organizations created and run by the blind, for the blind.

The Seeing Eye, Inc.
10 Washington Valley Road
P.O. Box 375
Morristown, NJ 07963
(973) 539-4425
info@seeingeye.org
www.seeingeye.org

The Seeing Eye (TSE) is the oldest guide dog school in the world. TSE breeds dogs specifically for the purpose of aiding people with disabilities, and provides instructional courses and training methods with one common goal: the empowerment of people who are blind.

The American Sighthound Field Association
3052 Mann Road
Blacklick, OH 43004
(614) 855-5067
president@asfa.org
www.asfa.org

The American Sighthound Field Association (ASFA) is a non-profit organization that provides guidelines for the sport of lure coursing in the United States.

The American Mixed Breed Obedience Registry
P.O. Box 223
Anoka, MN 55303
www.ambor.us

The American Mixed Breed Obedience Registry (AMBOR) is a registry for mixed-breed dogs seeking to ensure that they are able to fairly compete in obedience and dog agility.

Also Available from LaChance Publishing

LaChance Publishing's titles are available
everywhere fine books are sold.

Volume and institutional discounts are available.

The *Voices Of* Series

Packed with inspiring, informative true stories by individuals from all
walks of life who have been touched by major illness, the *Voices Of*
books are like support groups in book form. Each volume contains the
latest medical information and a comprehensive Resources section for
those seeking care.

"Poignant, insightful, moving... highly recommended."
Library Journal

Voices of Alcoholism

Voices of Alzheimer's

Voices of Autism

Voices of Bipolar Disorder

Voices of Breast Cancer

Voices of Caregiving

Voices of Lung Cancer

Voices of Multiple Sclerosis

Take Your Oxygen First

Protecting Your Health and Happiness
While Caring for a Loved One with Memory Loss

By Leeza Gibbons, Dr. James Huysman, and Dr. Rosemary Laird

Television host Leeza Gibbons and her family open their hearts to candidly share their experience of caring for Leeza's mother as she battled Alzheimer's disease, an ordeal that challenged the well being of an entire family. *Take Your Oxygen First* reveals how you can harness the power of the Three E's: *Education, Empowerment* and *Energy* to make the most of your own caregiving journey.

"*A message of hope pervades every page!*"
Larry King

Individuals diagnosed with life-threatening or chronic, debilitating ill-nesses face countless physical, emotional, social, spiritual, and financial challenges during their treatment and throughout their lives. The sup-port of family members, friends, and the community at large is essential to their successful recovery and their quality of life, and access to accu-rate and current information about their illnesses enables patients and their caregivers to make informed decisions about treatment and post-treatment care. Founded in 2005 by Debra LaChance, The Healing Project is dedicated to promoting the health and well-being of these individuals, developing resources to enhance their quality of life, and supporting the family members and friends who care for them. For more information about The Healing Project and its programs, please visit our website at www.thehealingproject.org.

For the duration of the printing and circulation of this book, for every book that is sold by LaChance Publishing, LaChance will contribute 100% of the net proceeds to The Healing Project, LLC. The Healing Project can be reached at 12 Warren Place, Brooklyn, NY 11217. The Healing Project is dedicated to promoting the health and well being of individuals challenged by life threatening or chronic illness and to developing resources to enhance their quality of life and the lives of their families. The Healing Project is a tax exempt organization as described in Revenue Code Section 501(c) (3).